THE RED-HAIRED ARCHAEOLOGIST

AMANDA HOPE HALEY

HARVEST HOUSE PUBLISHERS
EUGENE, OREGON

Cover design by Kyler Dougherty
Cover photo © ZU_09, sqback, yai112, LiliGraphie / gettyimages
Cover photo Polaroid by Amanda Hope Haley
Interior design by KUHN Design Group
Maps and illustrations by Michelle Pitts
Author photo on back cover by Matthew Stevens

For bulk, special sales, or ministry purchases, please call 1-800-547-8979.
Email: customerservice@hhpbooks.com

The Red-Haired Archaeologist Digs Israel
Copyright © 2021 Amanda Hope Haley
Photographs © Amanda Hope Haley
Published by Harvest House Publishers
Eugene, Oregon 97408
www.harvesthousepublishers.com

ISBN 978-0-7369-8093-7 (pbk.)
ISBN 978-0-7369-8094-4 (eBook)

Library of Congress Cataloging-in-Publication Data is on file at the Library of Congress, Washington, DC.

Printed in the United States of America

20 21 22 23 24 25 26 27 28 29 / VP-SK / 10 9 8 7 6 5 4 3 2 1

For all who long to see God's creation
and to know about the people who have lived in it

CONTENTS

MEET THE RED-HAIRED ARCHAEOLOGIST

I was first exposed to archaeology in the fifth grade when a teacher decided to prepare a unit on the science. She brought in plastic bins filled with layers of colorful dirt and tiny objects hidden in the homemade strata. It was raining outside that day, so we had to "dig" under the harsh fluorescents in the portable classroom. We had tiny instruments—miniature trowels, artists' brushes, tablespoon "shovels"—and strict instructions to keep ourselves and the classroom clean. My friend Charlie started tickling my ear with one of the brushes, and in my zeal to get away from him, I turned over my plastic "site." My cheeks flushed as red as my hair as the teacher scolded, "You're my quiet Little Red-Haired Girl, not a Pig-Pen!"

As filthy as I was when I arrived home that day, the rainbow stains were nothing compared to how I would look at the end of every dig day at the archaeological sites in Israel. Sometimes the dirt would pour out of my shoes, but usually it had blended with sweat and been ground into crevices not even a loofah could reach. No doubt, I was the Pig-Pen of Ashkelon in 2004, and I loved every dusty moment.

Growing up, I was certainly more princess than Pig-Pen. I delighted in baking fancy desserts and hated every moment of mowing the lawn. Even my sport of choice, swimming, was clean; I loved that no one could see me sweating during practices or events. So no one was more surprised than I was to discover my affinity for digging.

In the spring of 2001, I was a college sophomore and International Studies major working toward law school. Since Rhodes College has a Presbyterian heritage, all students were required to take four religion courses, and I had chosen biblical archaeology as my last one. During a weekend at home, I shared what I was learning with my parents and asked if I could go dig at Tel Rehov that summer with my adviser and Israel Finkelstein, one of Israel's most famous and controversial modern archaeologists. They agreed—if I could get a full scholarship to do so. One week later my trip was fully funded, and my dad and mom were wondering why on earth they had said yes to sending me to such a dangerous part of the world.

That summer, Israel was in the middle of the Second Intifada, a time of political unrest and violence between Israelis and Palestinians characterized by suicide bombings, bus bombings, kidnappings, targeted military attacks, and failed international interventions. The conflict was so bad that archaeological digs were canceled in Israel during the 2001 season. I was very sad and a little relieved (my parents were just relieved!), but the cancellation gave me the opportunity to date a guy named David Haley.

Three years later, I was married to David and studying biblical archaeology at Harvard University under Lawrence Stager, a scholar who could be thought of as the anti-Israel Finkelstein. (The two men had a public disagreement over whether or not kings David and Solomon were historical or legendary.[1] I often wondered if Harvard would have accepted me had I dug at Tel Rehov in 2001.) I was invited to dig at Ashkelon in 2004, during what was supposed to be the closing season. It was intense. We dug six days a week from five o'clock in the morning until noon. We would then shower, "do laundry" in the bathroom sink, eat lunch, and rest a bit before returning to the site to clean and catalog the day's finds. The day would end with just enough time for dinner and a phone call home before bedtime in a small room with two roommates.

The 2004 Ashkelon staff was small. We only dug in one grid that

A gufa (basket made from recycled tires), dustpan, and brush next to a wall I pickaxed.

Because most volunteers and staff members have the same brand of trowel, I had a friend personalize mine with my first initial.

season, so everyone knew and helped everyone else—and everyone did everything. In one day, I might start out pickaxing an area. Once it was down five-or-so centimeters (or however deep my supervisor told me to go), I'd smooth the area with my trowel and then sweep the loose dirt off the compacted dirt just below it. If something other than broken pottery sherds or bones was discovered, I'd use a tape measure

with leveling strings and a plumb bob to locate in three dimensions exactly where the object was buried, and then precisely draw it on a plan sheet.

The schedule was the same every dig day, but activities could change with every new object we uncovered. The worst days were those spent excavating the ancient streets. Every swing of the pickax would bring up the trash of the ancient world. We picked countless pottery sherds and broken animal bones out of the dirt, and then we had to scoop up the dirt, haul it out of the square, sift it, and finally wheelbarrow it to our own growing "trash heap" of excavated dirt adjacent to the grid. When the heavy work was over at the end of the day, we'd do a final sweep of the square, brushing loose dirt into dustpans so the site would be ready the next

Excavating the bottom of a bowl-lamp-bowl foundation deposit buried by the house's owners sometime around 1000 BCE. The date designation BCE means "before the common era" and is used by archaeologists instead of BC (before Christ) for various reasons, including the calculation that Jesus was actually born in 4 BCE, four years before the Christian calendar states. Likewise, archaeologists use CE (common era) instead of AD (anno domini, "in the year of our Lord").

morning. This monotonous, hot, heavy work taught me how susceptible fair-skinned, red-haired girls can be to intense dehydration that can lead to sunstroke.

My happiest memory of that first dig was excavating a perfectly preserved artifact. During the Iron Age, which roughly corresponds to the time when the land was ruled by Israelites (1200 BCE–586 BCE), Philistines would sometimes bury two unused bowls and a new lamp under the corners of their houses as a sort of blessing, just as we might dedicate a cornerstone to a new building. I had to lift the bowl-lamp-bowl foundation deposit out carefully using artist brushes and a nasal aspirator so the ancient pottery would not crack as it saw its first sunlight in 3,000 years.

But not everything that came out of the ground was inanimate. One day, as I was working next to a wall in the kitchen of an Iron Age house, I was chatting with a friend who was tracing a floor on the other side of that wall. We were both squatting (it is best not to sit on your bottom or rest on your knees while digging) when a scorpion wiggled out of the wall. My tall and stocky friend, who had seemed undaunted by anything all season, gave a high-pitched shriek as he performed the most magnificent land-based backstroke dive I've ever seen. I responded by lifting my trowel and calmly stabbing the furious little creature where it stood next to me with its tail raised. (My heroics are yet to be duplicated; 15 years later I was the one screaming as a yellow jacket crawled out of a balk.)

To enhance your reading experience, visit **www.redhaired archaeologist.com**. There you will find more than 200 color photographs taken during my trips to Israel!

In 2019, I made my less-than-glorious return to archaeological excavation at Tel Shimron. This was a new dig staffed by many of my 2004 friends and led by Daniel Master, a professor at Wheaton College and former assistant director of Harvard's Leon Levy Expedition to Ashkelon. At the age of 38, I was almost old enough to be the mother of the other volunteers on the dig. I had worried for months about being so much older than all the other volunteers. Would they accept me as a team member? Would I be physically up to the task of digging?

My square mates (Abby, Nick, Kaz, Max, me, and Avie) on our "stone throne" at the edge of Grid 39.

The answer to those questions would be yes—mostly. Surrounded by undergraduate and graduate students, I oscillated between being their "wise woman," addressing (if not answering) the theological and sometimes-philosophical questions they asked me, imagining cartoon characters who might appear in a children's version of the very book you are holding, and marveling at their love of "classic" music from the 1990s, which made me feel included and old at the same time. As we worked, they streamed that music on their iPhones thanks to unlimited wireless data plans; it was a constant reminder to me of how the world has changed in 15 years. We would never have dreamed of bringing our cell phones overseas in 2004; I had used a calling card and a hotel pay phone to talk to David each day!

The introduction of wireless music to the grid was just the beginning of how technology had revolutionized archaeology since I'd been at Ashkelon. The manual dig techniques I'd honed came back quickly, but the new instruments took me a while to understand and use. Gone were my hand-drawn plat maps, leveling strings, and plumb bobs; no longer did we handwrite bucket tags. In the middle of the grid stood a giant tripod that allowed us to take three-dimensional measurements of any depth, structure, or artifact using GPS. Each square supervisor had his or her own laptop to note finds as they came out of the ground, and we tagged them with barcodes from a tiny, dust-covered printer. Final photographs at the end of the season were taken by drones.

Fifteen years of new technology had made digging faster, easier, and (most importantly) more accurate. Fifteen years of life and its stresses had made me stiffer and heavier. When I woke up at 4:00 a.m. on my four-inch-thick foam mattress the morning of day three, I could barely move. For the first week, I constantly shifted between squatting, standing, and bending over to trowel or sweep the ground beneath me. I ran out of ibuprofen almost immediately. My plan of digging during the days and writing during the evenings immediately went out the window as I needed to sleep away my free time in hopes of feeling a bit better the next day. By the third week, thanks to cutting all carbohydrates, drinking nothing but water, and consuming a mega bottle of ibuprofen bought for me by one of my dear square mates, I could finally focus more on the dirt than on my aching neck, back, and legs.

An absolute requirement for every staff member and volunteer on an archaeological site is attention to detail. In the ancient world, civilizations often built directly on top of one another, creating layers of dirt, debris, and artifacts unique to each community. As all those layers stack on top of each other over millennia, a large mound is created called a *tel*. One must be able to see and feel the differences in the ground to know when occupation levels are changing. For example, if I am sweeping the loose, yellowish, ash-rich dirt out of an ancient fire pit, then I need to see and feel when I reach the

As I reported on social media that morning, "Off to a bad start for dig day 3. I basically can't feel my legs. This is the reality of excavation when you're waaaay out of practice!"

bottom of the pit, which is likely to be a different color and made of denser soil. If I keep digging through the bottom, then I'd be removing dirt from an earlier civilization's occupation and might damage as-yet-uncovered evidence of those residents.

At the bottom of one fire pit, I found evidence of an ancient floor. There was a thin, white substance that covered the bottom of the pit and could actually be traced up and out of the pit and across an ancient courtyard. By "tracing the floor" (using a trowel to carefully flake the dirt lying on top of the white substance up and off), archaeologists can see a layout of an ancient space. They can see what objects were dropped on the floor and can tell what activities may have happened on it. In an ancient kitchen, for example, one might find often-broken cooking pots, pieces of ovens, animal bones, and even seeds. From those artifacts, we can learn about the diets and cooking methods of the ancient homeowner.

One must dig cleanly in order to recognize the changes in dirt, and that takes time. Tracing a plastered floor, articulating a stone wall, and exhuming a corpse are all delicate tasks that can take days to complete; but dig seasons only last a few weeks each year, and there are thousands of years of civilizations yet to be uncovered in Israel and all over the rest of the world. The need for care and the shortage of time create tension between digging well and digging quickly. Archaeologists don't want to lose any valuable information, but we would like to learn as much as possible about a city each season.

In an ideal world, tels would be "strip excavated"—Islamic archaeologists would begin work at the top of the tel, excavating the whole area until they hit Byzantine artifacts. Then Byzantine scholars would take over until they reached Roman remains and handed the site off to Roman experts. And so on, and so on, until the tel was leveled. During each season, all sorts of scientists—biologists, botanists, epigraphers, geologists, and zoologists, to name a few—would be consulted on site. Tests would be run, photographs and videos would be taken, and money would never run out. But there isn't much about this world that is *ideal*. Time, money, and volunteers are all finite.

In the real world, one site is excavated by a team of scholars at the same time. After ground-penetrating radar has given experts an idea of what artifacts may lie below the surface, "chunks" are removed from the tel by heavy equipment in different areas down to different depths. Newer civilizations, such as Islamic and Byzantine, will be evidenced closer to the surface of the tel; older civilizations, such as those from the Iron, Bronze, and Chalcolithic ages, will typically need to have much more dirt removed before the staff and volunteers arrive to exhume artifacts. All time periods of a tel are excavated simultaneously each season by teams who have specialties in the civilizations they are digging.

Although artifacts of newer civilizations may be lost when backhoes make their first cuts into the side of a tel, there is one major perk

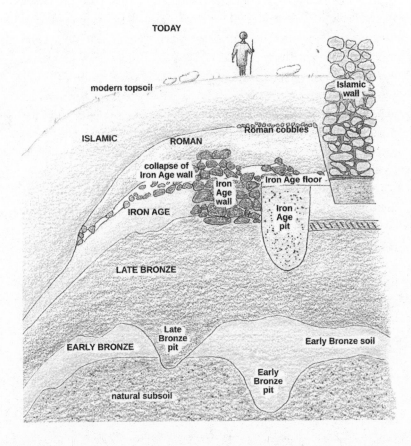

to "spot excavating": Parts of a tel remain untouched for decades and centuries. What we don't exhume today will remain *in situ* (that is, "in place" and undisturbed) for future archaeologists who will likely approach the same tel with more technology and more knowledge than we have today. If all layers of a tel were stripped away by one team of excavators at one point in time, then it would be practically impossible for future archaeologists to reinvestigate ancient cities when nothing remained of them in the dirt.

As all scientific fields are advancing, so does archaeology. Decades ago, excavators and scholars would have assumed that my white floor was simply plaster and been thrilled to catalog what artifacts were left on top of it, knowing they were all in use at the same time by the same people. But thanks to advancements in microbiology, specialists from the Weizmann Institute were able to see that the floors contained *phytoliths*, microscopic plant structures that remain after a plant decays and disappears. Scientists such as Steve Weiner can identify what plants were present on top of that floor thousands of years ago but that we can no longer see.[2] Remains may indicate what people and animals ate and drank, what fibers were spun and woven into garments, and what parasites lived with humans in those pre-antibacterial-soap days. What we can't see with a naked eye can tell archaeologists more about ancient civilizations than what we can see.

On the surface, digging for broken bowls, discarded animal bones, invisible plants, and the occasional necklace doesn't seem necessary or even useful. Why spend so much time and money excavating mundane objects when there are great treasures still undiscovered? With advancing technology that can make the unseen seen and biblical clues from God Himself, why haven't archaeologists found Noah's ark or Moses's ark of the covenant or Jesus's last wine glass? Surely all volunteers and staff members at a dig dream of their own "Indiana Jones" moments, but searching the world for one object isn't archaeology—it's treasure hunting.

If any of the Bible's Big Three artifacts were ever discovered, then most of the world would pay attention. Jews and Christians would make pilgrimages to see them, and we'd likely all marvel at just how wrong our individual visions of those objects were based on our Bible translations and traditional descriptions. But how would their discoveries benefit humanity beyond the spectacle of it all? Would seeing two-, three-, and five-thousand-year-old *things* help us better understand the ancient cultures into which God first breathed His Scriptures? Will they help us to know Him better?

True biblical archaeology, when practiced without a specific goal such as "prove the Flood happened," or "find God's seat," or "drink from the cup of Christ," teaches us about the people and societies of the ancient world. We can identify with the woman who cooked bread in her kitchen or the man who smelted copper, bronze, or iron into tools. We live mundane lives, so we are more likely to be impacted by the ancients' mundane lives than by history's spectacular oddities. When we understand their lives, we are more likely to connect with their stories and metaphors. We can feel the hunger and sorrow of the widow as she presses some of her last dough onto the side of her ancient oven to make a cake for Elijah (1 Kings 17:8-16); we can understand the heat and horror of the Hebrews' slavery when Egypt is likened to a crucible (1 Kings 8:51).

I invite you to come along with my family and me as we spend two weeks touring Israel, both ancient and modern. Together we will visit many archaeological sites and see artifacts that make the words of the Bible tangible. We will walk streets and shorelines where Jesus walked, imagining ourselves as His followers and wondering what He must think of modern Israel. We will enjoy the varied landscapes, endure oppressive dry heat, stand in maybe-too-many air-conditioned museums, and swim in three distinct "seas"—all while interacting with the "mundane" people of the land—Jewish and Muslim, Israeli and Palestinian. What begins as a quest to better understand the contexts and meanings of Scripture and better know the One who made them and us just might end with us having a better understanding of our neighbors and how Jesus would have us love them today.

CHAPTER 1

LOGISTICS IN MODERN ISRAEL

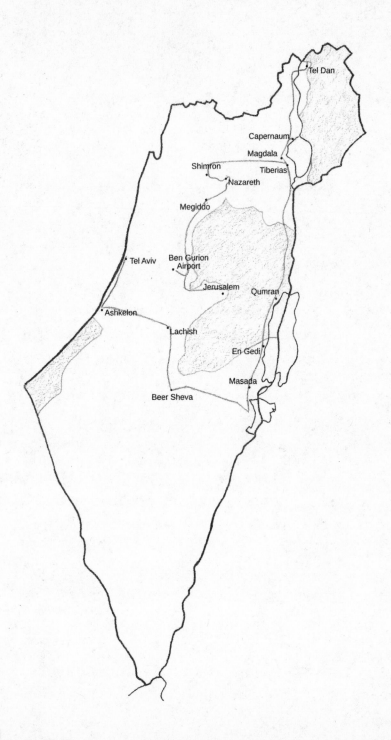

While I was at Harvard in the early 2000s, I worked for a small tour company called New England Sights. We did a lot of party planning for Boston elites and some vacation planning for out-of-towners. People would contact us through our website, the owner would design the ideal trip for them, and I would execute her plans. We provided beautiful vacations for companies and families to locations and events they could never have found themselves.

In the age of online travel sites, Yelp reviews, Waze maps, and Google Translate, it is tempting to think we can all craft our own vacations to exotic locales with just a few clicks. Technically, this is true, but it is far more time-consuming and accident-prone than taking a cruise or joining a bus tour where all of the logistics have been figured out for you by locals. If you are like me, and you don't want to be tied down to someone else's schedule or visit only the "usual" places where everyone goes, then you have to do your own research, reserve your own lodgings and transportation, and be your own guide. You also have to be ready to interact with people confidently and kindly.

GETTING TO ISRAEL

Row Buddy

Traveling to Israel from Chattanooga required twenty-two hours, four cities, three planes, a train, and an automobile. Patience, grace, and efficiency were helpful as I encountered countless other travelers and travel professionals. Most interactions were brief, but one of those people would be stuck in the seat beside me for the 11 hours it takes to fly from JFK to Tel Aviv.

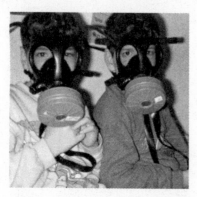

Lior and sibling during an air raid in 1991.

I boarded the plane and found my row buddy already in his aisle seat. He stood up and let me slide over to the window, then waited politely as I rummaged around for my electronics before stowing my carry-ons. I put out my hand and introduced myself to Lior, who was traveling from his new home in Boston to Haifa, where his mother had just had surgery. We talked nonstop for the next four or so hours about our plans in Israel, our lives back home, and world politics.

Lior and I are the same age, but he was born in Jerusalem and grew up in Haifa, while I am a Tennessean. We found ourselves discussing the first Gulf War (August 2, 1990, to February 28, 1991) and the strikes on Israel in the run-up to it, when we were both about nine years old. I didn't remember very much from that time period, other than CNN broadcasting the bombing of Israel and National Guardsmen talking to our classes when they returned home, but I had studied the war a bit in college. Lior's memory of the events surprised me: "I remember going down into the bomb shelter and putting on a gas mask, and then we got off school for a whole month. It was great as a third grader! No school for a whole month! Of course, my parents didn't explain to us exactly what was happening. It just seemed like a lot of spontaneous fun."

According to building codes, bomb shelters are required in all Israeli houses.

Airport Security

I haven't had the best luck with customs agents. When I was 17, my parents and I were returning to the US from London when we were told to enter the glass-walled interrogation room that was then called the Immigration and Naturalization Service (INS). "Don't worry," my dad told my mom and me, "I've been traveling a lot lately, so they probably just want to question me about it."

For 30 minutes, we waited in an otherwise-empty room for the armed, uniformed agent to call us up to the front where he "held court" from an elevated platform behind a six-foot-high wooden wall. After we approached, he looked down on us and asked, "Which one of you is Amanda?"

The color drained from my face, and my dad tried to take over: "She's my daughter. We are returning from London…"

"I wasn't talking to *you*," the agent bellowed. This would be the only time I ever saw my father tuck his metaphorical tail between his legs.

The agent started shifting papers and asking me identifying questions. It turned out that a girl fitting my physical description with my first and last name, my birthday, and a social security number one digit different from mine had gone missing in Arizona. When the customs agent had scanned my passport, the system had flagged me as the runaway and my parents as potential kidnappers!

Since that happened, I've developed a slight fear of customs agents. Twenty-one years later, as I approached the Israeli agent in Ben Gurion airport, I broke into a stress sweat. He was locked in an elevated glass box with a computer and scanning device (and a weapon, I assumed) that I could not see. I had to stand on my tiptoes to speak into and listen from the six-inch break in the glass. I slid him my passport and an official letter identifying me with the Tel Shimron excavation.

The first questions were normal: "Tell me your name. What is your business here? Are you excavating for a private group or a government group? Do you plan to go to any adjacent countries while you are in Israel?" But then he started telling me things about myself, as a charlatan fortune-teller might do.

"You are from Tennessee."

"Yes."

"But you've never lived in Tennessee."

I was flummoxed. "Well, I live there now. And I grew up there."

He interrupted me with something that wasn't quite statement or question: "You were born and raised in Tennessee."

"Yes."

"But, madam, *you have no accent!*"

I stammered, "Thank you?"

He stared.

"Well, my dad's family is from Virginia, so maybe that's why?"

He asked me more about the excavation and my educational background, and then quietly slid the visa into my passport and waved me toward the crossing. I quit the stress sweating sometime that evening.

Six weeks later, as I was preparing to leave Israel, I remembered just how difficult it had been to get out of the country in 2004. For the Ashkelon excavation, I had traveled into Israel with a group, but I left by myself. That raised the first red flag. The customs agents opened my luggage and searched it in front of me, and then I was pulled out of the regular security line. A pin in my right ankle set off their highly sensitive metal detectors, so I was patted down while a specialist investigated my shoes. Then the questioning began. I sat in a windowless room as multiple people came in asking me the same questions:

"Why are you in Israel?"

"Are you taking anything home with you from the dig?"

"Why are you leaving Israel before other members of your group?"

"Did anyone give you anything to transport?"

"Did you travel to another country at any time while you had an Israeli visa?"

Luckily, I'd celebrated my twenty-third birthday during the dig, and someone had given me copies of some drawings from Ashkelon's Grid 38. I pulled them out and explained to each interviewer what I had been working on. The investigation took two hours to complete, but El Al (Israel's national airline) held the plane for me. I made it back to JFK just in time to make my connection home.

While this process sounds scary, I mostly remember that everyone was so kind to me. Before each question, they would apologize for making me uncomfortable and explain they were trying to make sure my flight would be safe. At no point did anyone believe I was anything other than a graduate student and dig volunteer (I don't think!), but the Israelis' vigilance is why El Al is one of the safest airlines in the world.

Thankfully, I didn't have the same trouble leaving in 2019. I had done the opposite on this trip—I had entered alone and was exiting with a group. My husband, David, and my parents, Ross and Dana, had never been to Israel; so they joined me for the tour portion of my trip. We didn't have any problems crossing back into the US either; no one thought I'd been kidnapped this time!

TRAVELING THROUGH ISRAEL

Driving

It never ceases to amaze me that a US passport allows me to drive a car in any country. Although their symbols and lines are different, their signs may not be in English, and they may drive on the left side of the road from the right side of the car, I can hop into any international driver's seat and go.

The day before my family arrived in Tel Aviv, I had ridden on a bus from Tel Shimron to the airport with several other volunteers including Abby, one of my square mates. She needed to get to Jerusalem before she began working on yet another excavation the following day, and I couldn't check into my Tel Aviv hotel room until 5:00 p.m. that evening. We decided to drive the 30 minutes between Tel Aviv and Jerusalem and spend the day roaming around the Old City. I would drop her off at her hostel that evening before returning to Tel Aviv.

Not only was I happy for the company on my one totally unplanned day in Israel, but I was in need of a navigator. I need time to adjust when I enter a vehicle other than Dory, our 2014 Subaru Forester. I may brake too firmly or misjudge blind spots for the first few miles until I have a feel for the new-to-me machine. I had rented a Mitsubishi Eclipse (which is a small SUV and not the sports car I envisioned and feared as the clerk handed me the keys!), knowing it would be heavy laden with four adults and floor-to-ceiling luggage for most of the trip. But I did not expect another encounter with technology. Abby and I sat in the airport parking structure for at least 30 minutes trying to figure out all the buttons and inputs. This would be my first experience with Android Auto, lane assistance, start-stop technology, and something called SafeCar.

SafeCar is an aftermarket anti-theft system that has drastically reduced car thefts in Israel. All Israeli cars—personal and rentals— come equipped with a small keypad near the steering column. Before the driver inserts the key into the ignition, she must enter a four-digit code followed by the star. It is a simple concept, but it was difficult to insert in the middle of my 23-year-long muscle-memorized routine of sitting down, buckling my seat belt, and inserting the key. Up until the day I turned the car back in, David would yell at me, "Punch in the code!" every time we entered the car.

Abby and I got out of the parking garage slowly but with no problems. My first drive to Jerusalem was exciting and easy with her running the navigation and sound systems. We found two-hour, not-parallel parking in Jerusalem near a lovely restaurant, Etz Café, where we ate our first nonkosher meal in weeks and enjoyed a cool August morning at a sidewalk table. Then we returned to the car.

Upon entering and without thinking, I inserted the key before typing in the four-digit code. The car beeped angrily, so I removed the key, opened and closed the driver's door, and waited ten seconds as the rental clerk had told me to do. I am certain I did it correctly the next time, but SafeCar beeped at me again. For the next five minutes, Abby and I both tried to figure out what was going wrong; as panic set in, we even tried to enter the numbers in reverse because Hebrew letters read from right to left (although their numbers read left-to-right, and we knew that). Inexplicably, the car started rolling backward, making a circling angry taxi driver think we were leaving. But it never actually turned on. By the time the car's back end was halfway into traffic, that taxi driver stopped to help us. He and Abby pushed the car back into the parking space, and I set the emergency brake. I called the car rental company, they reset the SafeCar system remotely, and it worked perfectly from that moment forward.

The next day I confidently walked into Ben Gurion airport. I knew where I was going, I'd had almost 24 hours without a car mishap, and my family was arriving! We got settled in the car into what would be our permanent spaces for the whole trip: David next to me up front, my dad behind me, and my mom beside him. The luggage was in the back, stacked to the ceiling, and my father and mother were squished with a couple of bags in the backseat between them.

> When you are navigating in Israel, use Waze. It was invented in Israel, so its maps of streets, alleyways, and traffic are significantly better than the other services we tried.

Pulling into Tel Aviv rush-hour traffic, I learned three things quickly: Israeli drivers are aggressive, I had a significant blind spot on the passenger side in the back, and Israeli roundabouts don't have inner and outer lanes as American ones do—everyone just tumbles in together no matter which lane they are coming from or turning into. The rules of the road may not be too different from US highways, but the driving culture is. There is no time for timidity when everyone around you has pushed the gas pedal before the light has turned green, and a "safe distance" must be less than a car length if you don't want to be constantly cut off and sideswiped.

By far my biggest driving snafu started between two roundabouts in a residential area of downtown Nazareth. We were trying to get to the Basilica of the Annunciation (where tradition states that God's messenger, Gabriel, told Mary that she would soon be carrying Jesus), and our GPS kept telling me to turn down a tight-looking alleyway that wound between ancient three- and four-story buildings. We passed by the alley, all agreeing there must be a better way to get to the church. At the next roundabout, the GPS sent us back by the same alley, again telling us to turn. Then the next roundabout turned us around again with the GPS's ever-angrier-sounding demand that we turn! I hesitated. My dad said, "Let's go for it," just as David said, "Nuh-uh." With a car flying up behind me, I turned.

I'm not sure when my mom started crying. It could have been in the first ten seconds when a little red sports car flew by us going the opposite direction, or maybe it was when a local gave us a strange look as we approached his stoop. The alley had been curving left and right as we drove down at a steep grade—and it was getting noticeably narrower. The Arabic-speaking gentleman walked up to my window and asked where we were going in internationally recognizable hand signals. I pointed up to the church's spire. He furrowed his brow and then nodded vigorously that we should continue down and to the left instead of reversing to the right and driving out.

We kept going, and the alley narrowed.

We flipped in the side-view mirrors, and the alley narrowed more.

Our tires rubbed against a bottom step, and there was a column— the base to someone's second-story expansion—blocking the middle of our path.

We were stuck.

As I sat there thinking, *This is going to be expensive to correct*, and imagining a helicopter with magnets for landing skids lifting us straight out of this predicament, my dad sucked himself in and wiggled himself out of the backseat. He continued down the alley on foot and quickly found a bar where men were playing cards and the bartender was wearing a Nike shirt. The bartender spoke English, and he walked back with my dad to the SUV.

But before they arrived, a mother appeared with six children. The boys were running circles upon and around the vehicle as my father and the bartender appeared. The man and woman spoke to each other in Arabic and got on their cell phones. To the right of the SUV were four parking spaces crammed full with five cars, and one by one the owners came down to move them. The children were shooed upstairs into their home, and what ensued was the most complex expression of a sliding-block puzzle in which I've ever participated. Somehow, we all got the SUV turned around and the cars back in their parking places.

We made it to the church just in time for a Latin mass to begin outside the cave where tradition says Gabriel appeared to Mary.

Throughout it all, my father remained cool as a cucumber. He decided that on our way out he would walk ahead of the car just in case we met another vehicle around one of the tight turns. As David, my mom, and I slowly climbed up the alleyway behind my pedestrian father, the Mitsubishi's start-stop technology repeatedly shut off the engine and then lurched forward, to which my distraught mother responded, "Don't hit your father!"

It took half an hour, a literal village, and my mother's constant prayers, but we made it out of that Nazareth alleyway without a scratch. As I took my first full breath since turning down that road, I asked my family, "Do you think we are done with Nazareth?" We all agreed that we were, and I headed toward the highway, only to find parking for the basilica two blocks away from our adventure.

Lodging and Dining

When you book a hotel in Israel, you'll notice they offer boarding options, meaning you can pay up front for one, two, or three meals per day. This is nothing like free continental or grab-and-go breakfasts offered at some express hotels in the US; every meal is a gigantic buffet offering all types of food at all times of day. If you are feeling traditional, you can ask the staff to make you a fresh pancake for breakfast, but then pile pizza, pasta, casserole, cheeses, breads, and at least five different salads alongside it. Have some complimentary kosher wine on Shabbat, and get ready to stand in long lines for the espresso machines every other day of the week.

Aside from a fresh fish staring at you from your breakfast plate next to a slice of roast beef and fingerling potatoes on some mornings, the hardest thing to get used to is eating kosher. Meat and dairy will never appear in the same meal—so forget about a cheeseburger—and all shellfish and pork products—including everyone's favorite artery-hardener, bacon—are off the menu entirely.

Don't think you always have to eat at a hotel. Israel has some delicious, stylish, and award-winning restaurants. While visiting Akko, a largely Arab city on the Mediterranean just north of Haifa, another one of my square mates, Avie, and I had our first restaurant meals in Israel. We had traveled to the city with most of the other Tel Shimron

The Crusader fortress at Akko.

volunteers that weekend to tour the Crusader sites. Avie had never seen the Mediterranean Sea before, and I was happy to go down to the golden beach with her and take some pictures of this memorable day in her life. While we were walking along the coast, I noticed a seafood restaurant called Mina overhanging the sea's edge. Deciding we'd both seen enough old things for a while and wanting some comfort and fresh seafood, we walked over and got an outdoor table. She had their fresh fish of the day, I had a pot full of mussels, and we shared 13 small salads.

When we sat down, we figured we had a little over an hour to eat and walk back to the bus. Unbeknownst to us, the restaurant expected we would spend at least two hours eating. Service was kind but incredibly slow (which I would appreciate in any other situation). We had barely received our seafood when it was time to panic: We needed the check immediately so we wouldn't miss the bus. Avie went inside to try to get someone's attention while I boxed up our food and got my credit card ready.

While digging in my purse, a particularly strong gust of wind caused the canopy over our table to collapse on the right side. Avie hadn't been able to get anyone's attention, but that dramatic crash certainly did!

I texted the volunteer coordinator and told her what had just happened. She responded, "That is hilarious and horrifying! We will wait for you."

CHAPTER 2

FIGHTING PHILISTINES ON THE MEDITERRANEAN SEA

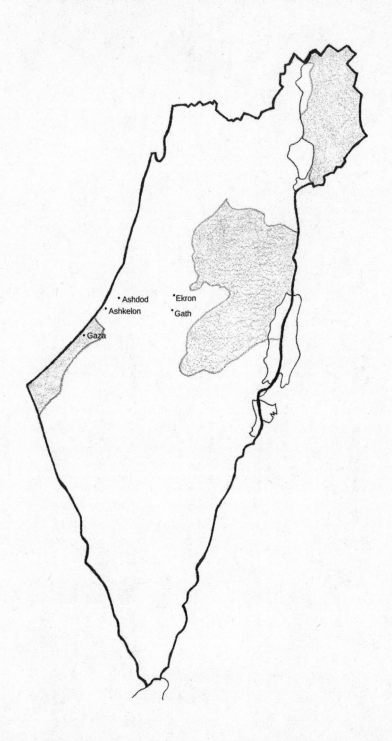

As we stepped out of the airport in Tel Aviv, Israel met all of my family's expectations. It is hot, almost unbearably sunny, and there's little vegetation in sight. Israel's famed White City is a concrete jungle, but shortly after turning south, the scenery changes to Mediterranean paradise. Palm trees dot the sky, and to our right is the bluest blue I've ever seen. The Israeli seaside reminds me of the French Riviera as depicted in *To Catch a Thief*; and for the first time in his life, David sees the color *azure* outside of a crayon box. We cannot wait to stand in that clear, beautiful water. But after 22 hours of travel, David and my parents will need naps before we can do that.

The modern city of Ashkelon isn't exactly a resort town, but it is a wonderful place for a beach vacation. People are out walking, enjoying the hot sun and cool breezes off the Mediterranean. Ice-cream stands on the sand sell kosher treats with dairy desserts in one case and non-dairy in the next, just in case you keep kosher and ate meat at your last meal. Sidewalks are wide and streets are wider in neighborhoods of mostly one-story, white-stucco homes with palm tree landscaping. The modern city center boasts a few skyscrapers—maybe ten stories each—among its shopping malls, street-front shops, and movie theaters. It looks and feels a lot like any Southern California coastal city.

This photograph of the ancient port was taken in 2004. The site was not excavated that year, but many of its formerly excavated walls are visible under a
protective mesh. After Ashkelon's closing season in 2016, the area was backfilled for visitors' safety.

Founded ca. 1950 BCE by the Canaanites, ancient Ashkelon was
the oldest and largest-known seaport in the area, home to 15,000 people. One hundred years later, the inhabitants built the oldest-known
arched city gate in the world (parts of which still stand two stories high),
city wall, rampart, and moat. The city was conquered by the Egyptians
ca. 1550 BCE, and then by the Philistine "Sea Peoples" in 1175 BCE.
Ashkelon thrived until the Babylonian King Nebuchadnezzar sacked
and burned the city in 604 BCE, exiling its prominent residents to
other parts of the Babylonian Empire. Eighteen years later, he would
do the same to Jerusalem (2 Kings 25:8-12).

The Bible doesn't tell us a lot about Ashkelon—it is usually just a
name rattled off in a list with the other four cities of the Philistine Pentapolis (Gath, Ekron, Ashdod, and Gaza)—but a 30-year-long excavation
of the tel revealed a wealthy, technologically advanced, and internationally connected port city that was home to strong and frequent enemies
of Israel during the times of the Judges and the United Monarchy.

FOUR EXCAVATED CITIES

The Philistines built their nation around five capital cities—Ashkelon, Gath, Ekron, Ashdod, and Gaza—after immigrating from southern Europe.[1] As we can see from what remains of those Iron Age cities, the people set to work building lives that looked a lot like those of their Canaanite and Israelite neighbors and enemies. They erected houses like their neighbors'; planted, wove, and brewed beer as their neighbors did; and worshiped many gods as the Canaanites and Egyptians had.

The four northern cities of Ashkelon, Gath, Ekron, and Ashdod are all in modern Israel. Their archaeological sites form a rough circle, each city an average of 35 minutes by car from its neighbors. Starting in Ashkelon, a counterclockwise tour of the sites can be completed in one very full day.

A Canaanite "Golden Calf" in Ashkelon

The Leon Levy Expedition ran excavations at Ashkelon from 1985 to 2016.[2] Now that the digs have ended and most of the grid has been backfilled with dirt for visitors' safety, it is easy to walk among the ruins, touch the city walls, look down into the ancient port, and imagine

The site of the discovery of the first golden calf

The first photograph, taken in 2004, shows the Canaanite gate after excavation but before restoration. The second photograph, taken in 2019, shows the same gate that has been reconstructed for both preservation of the original materials and education of the visitors.

working and playing—and worshiping—among the Canaanites and Philistines.

A small black-and-white sign with a drawing of a calf is stuck into the side of the Canaanite wall's rampart, marking an important discovery. It is easy to miss even if you are looking for it, and it is downright perplexing if no one is there to explain it. In that spot, the first Canaanite "golden calf" was found in its own clay shrine inside a 1600 BCE sanctuary just right of the city gate. The calf could stand easily on an adult's open hand, and his bronze body was once overlain with silver (contrary to our Bible-informed expectations, not every calf idol was gold!). To the Canaanite worshiper, this little guy likely represented either their god of storms (Ba'al Saphon) or their god of seafarers (Ba'al Hadad).

Canaanites, Egyptians, Philistines—basically everyone except the Israelites—liked to make idols and worship gods. Canaanite gods were all associated with an animal that the god would ride; for example, the god El rode a bull while his divine son, Ba'al, rode a calf. But an image of the god himself was not always necessary. Worshipers might mold his mount as a kind of ancient *icon* used to direct the owner to worship the space above it, as today's Orthodox Christians use their icons as constant reminders to focus their attention on God. The icon itself isn't worshiped as an idol would be; rather, it helps to direct worship.

In the Bible, golden calves appear when the Israelites are straying from God and tempted toward the worship of indigenous gods. The two best examples occur in Exodus 32 and 1 Kings 12:

> Now when the people saw that Moses delayed coming down from the mountain, the people gathered together to Aaron, and said to him, "Come, make us gods that shall go before us; for as for this Moses, the man who brought us up out of the land of Egypt, we do not know what has become of him."

> And Aaron said to them, "Break off the golden earrings which are in the ears of your wives, your sons, and your daughters, and bring them to me." So all the people broke off the golden earrings which were in their ears, and

brought them to Aaron. And he received the gold from their hand, and he fashioned it with an engraving tool, and made a molded calf.

Then they said, "This is your god, O Israel, that brought you out of the land of Egypt!"

So when Aaron saw it, he built an altar before it. And Aaron made a proclamation and said, "Tomorrow is a feast to the Lord." Then they rose early on the next day, offered burnt offerings, and brought peace offerings; and the people sat down to eat and drink, and rose up to play (Exodus 32:1-6).

[King Jeroboam] asked advice, made two calves of gold, and said to the people, "It is too much for you to go up to Jerusalem. Here are your gods, O Israel, which brought you up from the land of Egypt!" And he set up one in Bethel, and the other he put in Dan (1 Kings 12:28-30).

In both cases, the Israelites are separating themselves from their own worship traditions and mingling with non-Israelites. Moses and the Hebrews have left Egypt behind only to wander among and struggle against Canaanite tribes; Jeroboam and the ten northern tribes of Israel have separated themselves from God's temple in Jerusalem and are trying to figure out how to worship God from a new place. Both groups violate God's command against making graven images as the Hebrews make a calf out of some earrings, and the northern tribes build new temples at Dan and Bethel and put a calf in each. Even if God's people were making calf icons to direct their worship to their unseen God as their pagan neighbors sometimes did for their gods, God's people are ignoring His command not to make graven images, no matter how big they were or how the Israelites intended to use them. An icon itself wasn't worshiped, but it was still prohibited by God's Law (Exodus 20:4-6).

So where did God's people get the idea to cast metal calves? Cows were really only good for sacrifice in Israelite religion (Leviticus 9:3,8), so they weren't inherently worship-worthy. Ashkelon's calf proves that Canaanites were using bovine idols in their worship practices at the same time that the Hebrews were wandering near them; and the Egyptians from whom they had fled worshiped Hathor, a fertility goddess often depicted with a cow's head. By the time Jeroboam made his idols (as much as half a millennium after Aaron's was cast), calf iconography was well known to all the Israelites and thoroughly hated by God.

As I read the Exodus story of Aaron taking some earrings from the Hebrews, melting the metals down, and casting the golden calf, I can't help but picture Cecil B. DeMille's cinematic masterpiece, *The Ten Commandments*.[3] As the director depicted the scene, 12 bare-chested men carry a life-sized, golden calf wearing an Egyptian-style crown among dancing, singing, new-wine-drinking, fornicating Hebrews. A woman is almost "sacrificed" to the calf as another woman climbs upon its back and writhes (in a polite, 1956 kind of way). Certainly, DeMille intended to evoke thoughts of hedonism, excess, and orgies while keeping his actors clothed.

Part of the reason his interpretations are so engrained in Western imaginings of the golden calf may be the scenes' voiceovers. DeMille himself narrates the film using the same tone to speak his own scripted words as he does actual verses from the Bible. Viewers must have Exodus 32 open in front of them while watching the film to distinguish between holy Scripture and cinematic fiction because he blends the two so well!

The discovery of Ashkelon's calf offers Bible readers a geographically, historically, and religiously contextualized physical example of what the Bible might be describing (as opposed to a Technicolor-dyed, celluloid-captured human idea). Its existence prompts us to ask, "What if DeMille got the Exodus all wrong? What if Western society has missed the point of this biblical passage because Hollywood made it an *iconic* story (pun most definitely intended)?"

Imagine for a moment that you are Aaron—the priest the Bible scantly describes, and not the bumbling weakling DeMille portrays. Moses, the man who has led you out of Egypt, has been gone over a month, and there is no sign he will return. But you believe that God is on top of Mount Sinai. As the Hebrews around you get restless and are wondering if Moses will ever return, if they've made a bad choice leaving the cruel stability of Egypt, and if God has abandoned them entirely, you feel the need to act. Would you, a priest of God, so quickly abandon your faith? Or is it more likely that you would try to call God down from that mountain yourself, thinking Moses has failed? Would you gather the only remaining metal—maybe a few gallons' worth of earrings—and try to get His attention a different way?

By hypothesizing that Aaron was trying to call God back down to them—by making Him a seat as the Canaanites would make a calf-seat for Ba'al and as the Hebrews themselves would make a cheru-bim seat for God in Exodus 37—instead of giving the Hebrews an inanimate object to worship like Egypt's Hathor, we can identify with the Hebrews' sin instead of writing their blunder off as something we obviously know better than to do ourselves. An important moral of the story—that humanity lacks faith in and patience for God—is easier to recognize apart from Cecil B. DeMille's scene of wild paganism. Humans, ancient and modern, have always found ways to justify breaking God's laws, but more often we do it with subtle reasoning or peer pressure than with total conversion to another culture's religion.

Philistine "Giants" in Gath

Moving counterclockwise around the four northern cities of the ancient Philistine Pentapolis, we next come to the Philistine city of Gath at a modern archaeological site called Tel es-Safi. In 1996, a team of archaeologists led by Aren M. Maeir of Bar-Ilan University began a long-term excavation of the site.[4]

Gath is halfway between Ashkelon and Jerusalem, and it has been continuously occupied since the fifth millennium BCE. Gath was in the middle of an important ancient trade route, so the city was large, wealthy, and strategically important to all conquering empires of the ancient world. Because it was sieged and destroyed several times, a lot of material culture remains in the dirt. Archaeologists have been able to reconstruct the daily lives of Gath's first-millennium BCE citizens by the tools, weapons, pottery, art, and buildings they left behind.

Gath's most famous Iron Age citizen is probably Goliath, the so-called giant killed by David in 1 Samuel 17:

> A champion went out from the camp of the Philistines, named Goliath, from Gath, whose height was six cubits and a span [almost ten feet]. He had a bronze helmet on his head, and he was armed with a coat of mail, and the weight of the coat was five thousand shekels [126 pounds] of bronze. And he had bronze armor on his legs and a bronze javelin between his shoulders. Now the staff of his spear was like a weaver's beam, and his iron spearhead weighed six hundred shekels [15 pounds]; and a shield-bearer went before him (verses 4-7).

According to the Masoretic text of the Hebrew Bible, which is the first complete Hebrew text of the Old Testament ever discovered, Goliath was almost ten feet tall. However, the Greek Septuagint text of the Hebrew Bible, which is about 1,000 years older than the Masoretic text, says Goliath was six and a half feet tall. This discrepancy raises the question, Was more information lost in translation from Hebrew to Greek or lost during a millennium of scribes copying and recopying the Hebrew? Goliath was a big guy no matter which number is correct, but was he "The Gronk" big or can't-stand-up-in-my-house big? Was David, who had never before worn armor (1 Samuel 17:39), fighting against a seasoned warrior or a mythical creature?

I was surprised to realize that the Bible—no matter which text—never actually calls Goliath "giant." He is described as a tall, strong, fearsome warrior, but there is nothing to indicate that he himself lived at the top of a beanstalk, owned a blue ox named Babe, or sold frozen and canned vegetables. But one of his fellow citizens might have been. In the next book of the Bible, 2 Samuel, we read about some other Philistines identified as "the sons of the giant":

> When the Philistines were at war again with Israel, David and his servants with him went down and fought against the Philistines; and David grew faint. Then Ishbi-Benob, who was one of the sons of *the giant*, the weight of whose bronze spear was three hundred shekels, who was bearing a new sword, thought he could kill David. But Abishai the

son of Zeruiah came to his aid, and struck the Philistine and killed him. Then the men of David swore to him, saying, "You shall go out no more with us to battle, lest you quench the lamp of Israel."

Now it happened afterward that there was again a battle with the Philistines at Gob. Then Sibbechai the Hushathite killed Saph, who was one of the sons of *the giant.* Again there was war at Gob with the Philistines, where Elhanan the son of Jaare-Oregim the Bethlehemite killed the brother of Goliath the Gittite, the shaft of whose spear was like a weaver's beam.

Yet again there was war at Gath, where there was a man of great stature, who had six fingers on each hand and six toes on each foot, twenty-four in number; and he also was born to *the giant.* So when he defied Israel, Jonathan the son of Shimea, David's brother, killed him.

These four were born to *the giant* in Gath, and fell by the hand of David and by the hand of his servants (2 Samuel 21:15-22, emphasis added).

According to most English translations of 2 Samuel 2:15-21, several Philistine fighters—but not Goliath himself—were "sons of the giant." The Hebrew word that our translations record as "giant" is *Rapha,* which some try to connect to the Rephaim ("giants") of Genesis. However, it is just as (if not more) likely that *Rapha* was the father's name and should not be translated but transliterated, as it is in the Berean Study Bible, the New International Version, and The Voice Bible, and as most other English translations footnote it. Gath's material culture supports this idea because "all Philistine skeletal remains discovered so far have shown absolutely no evidence that the people were larger or different from normal-sized people."[5] Giant bones may still be out there, waiting to be found, but recent discoveries from Gaza agree that the city's inhabitants were of normal size.

During the 2019 excavation season at Gath, archaeologists unexpectedly uncovered a new layer of civilization that they date to the eleventh century BCE, roughly when David would have killed Goliath. All of the buildings in that layer were made from significantly larger materials than later structures. For example, building stones were up to two meters long instead of the usual half meter, and the city itself had a footprint twice the size of most of its contemporary neighbors'. Imagine if all of the houses in a neighborhood had their red bricks replaced by gray cinderblocks while maintaining the same square footage. The change in materials would be noticeable, but no Titans would have been necessary during construction.

The size differences may indicate that the older Philistines building this eleventh-century city were retaining the architectural traditions of the Aegean civilizations from where they came. What they built was *alien* to the Israelites, in the sense that it was from another country, not another species. The uniquely large architecture at Gath, combined with the Philistines' general reputations as fierce warriors, could have started the tradition that Goliath was a giant even though Scripture doesn't call him one.

The exaggerated ways the tradition has depicted both men (for David was likely not a skinny teenager as art paints him but a strong shepherd in his twenties) have resulted in a well-used and sometimes-trite metaphor designed to explain the success of a weakling in the face of impossible odds. The all-too-familiar "miracle" of David's win over a superhuman can obscure important details of the story. God had gifted David with a set of skills that made him not only able to win a battle but later to rule a kingdom. He was smart enough to avoid wearing ill-fitting, restrictive armor; he was strong enough to carry five sizable stones (not just pebbles) and swing one over his head with the velocity of a shot put and the accuracy of a bullet; he was agile enough to evade the skilled jabs of a seasoned warrior; and, most importantly, he was faithful enough to his God to confidently fight in His name when others were afraid. This wasn't a battle of the weak versus the strong, or the small versus the big, or even the young versus the old. It was an example of how God defies expectations.

Temple Furniture in Ekron

The next stop on the counterclockwise tour of ancient Philistia lands us at Tel Miqne, the site of ancient Ekron excavated by Trude

Dothan of Hebrew University and Seymour Gitin of the W.F. Albright Institute of Archaeological Research between 1981 and 1996. Like Ashkelon and Gath, Ekron was a bustling city during the Iron Age (when they would have been fighting with Saul and David). Their buildings and artwork also reflected the Philistine people's Aegean heritage.

In a large, two-story cultic building with elaborate entrances, interior columns, and a circular hearth paved with pebbles, excavators found three bronze wheels, each with eight spokes, that would have supported a *laver stand*. In the Aegean world, the wheels were attached to square, metal stands topped with water basins or "lavers" where offerings were kept. Such water stands were also present in Solomon's temple:

> Hiram then crafted 10 bronze moveable stands. Each water stand was 6 feet long, 6 feet wide, and 4½ feet high. The stands had side panels and panels between the crossbars. On the panels between the crossbars there were lions, oxen, and winged creatures. There was a pedestal over the crossbars that would support the basin, and there were garlands of ornaments below the lions and oxen. There were 4 bronze wheels and 4 bronze axles for each stand. The 4 legs of each stand also had 4 bases. There were bases with garlands on all sides below the basin (1 Kings 7:27-30 THE VOICE).

Ekron's water stand was the first example of a wheeled cult stand found in Israel and would have been in use around the time Solomon's temple was being prepared in the mid-tenth century BCE.[6] King Hiram, whom the Bible credits with creating the stands, was the king of Tyre, another Mediterranean society with strong ties to the Aegean. Among Philistine ruins, we get a glimpse of the type of furniture that would have been used to give sacrifices and offerings to Israel's God.

Temple Columns in Ashdod

Excavations at Ashdod-Yam, the last stop on our tour of the four northern capitals of the Philistines' Pentapolis, are mostly in their infancy. Small areas of the site were dug between 1968 and 1970, but little else was done until the summer of 2019, when Tel Aviv University spearheaded a new excavation that will hopefully run for a minimum of five seasons.[7]

Bible readers don't hear "Ashdod" and immediately think of specific Bible stories or characters as they do with Gath (Goliath) and Gaza (Samson). It is most famous for a story told in 1 Samuel 5–6, where God's ark of the covenant is taken into the Philistine temple after a battle with the Israelites:

> Then the Philistines took the ark of God and brought it from Ebenezer to Ashdod. When the Philistines took the ark of God, they brought it into the house of Dagon and set it by Dagon. And when the people of Ashdod arose early in the morning, there was Dagon, fallen on its face to the earth before the ark of the LORD. So they took Dagon and set it in its place again. And when they arose early the next morning, there was Dagon, fallen on its face to the ground before the ark of the LORD. The head of Dagon and both the palms of its hands were broken off on the threshold; only Dagon's torso was left of it. Therefore neither the priests of Dagon nor any who come into Dagon's house tread on the threshold of Dagon in Ashdod to this day.
>
> But the hand of the LORD was heavy on the people of Ashdod, and He ravaged them and struck them with tumors, both Ashdod and its territory. And when the men of Ashdod saw how it was, they said, "The ark of the God of Israel must not remain with us, for His hand is harsh toward us and Dagon our god." Therefore they sent and gathered to themselves all the lords of the Philistines, and said, "What shall we do with the ark of the God of Israel?" And they answered, "Let the ark of the God of Israel be carried away to Gath." So they carried the ark of the God of Israel away (1 Samuel 5:1-8).

But Ashdod will likely prove to be an abundant site, and it is already revealing impressive fortifications from the Iron Age, when its inhabitants would have been at war with David, and the ark of the covenant would have come into their city. The Bible reader can only hope that a fallen statue of the Philistine god, Dagon, might be found there!

ONE ENDURING CRISIS

The four northern cities of the Philistine Pentapolis are most often associated with David's military exploits in their area during the Iron Age. But 13 kilometers south of Ashkelon is the final capital city, Gaza, known for a Late Bronze Age judge named Samson.

Gaza in the Bible

You know the story. Israel, and particularly the tribe of Dan, has been under Philistine oppression for a generation when a messenger of the Lord tells a formerly barren woman that Samson is coming. He is to be a Nazirite, the messenger tells her, meaning he must never drink wine, cut his hair, or touch unclean stuff such as corpses and foreign women (Judges 13). Samson goes on to marry a Philistine, abandon her, get mad that she's remarried, and then kill 1,000 Philistines with nothing but a donkey's jawbone. The Philistines back off—because this guy is clearly crazy, right?—and Samson judges Israel for 20 years (Judges 14–15).

At some point and for some unknown reason, Samson is in Gaza one day and decides to visit a brothel. The Philistine men lie in wait to murder him, but Samson slips out of the brothel at midnight, picks up their city gate, and moves it from the edge of the city where it had been to the very center of the city. The Philistines knew he was a tough guy, but now they have witnessed his superhuman strength (Judges 16:1-3).

One last time, Samson gets involved with a woman. This time it is Delilah from the Valley of Sorek, the border between the tribe of Dan and the Philistines. The Philistines bribe her to find out the source of Samson's strength so they can capture him, torture him, and take him down to Gaza. She discovers that it is his uncut hair, which resulted from his Nazirite vows. The Philistines celebrate his capture at the temple of their god, Dagon, where Samson then kills them all:

So it happened, when their hearts were merry, that they said, "Call for Samson, that he may perform for us." So they called for Samson from the prison, and he performed for them. And they stationed him between the pillars. Then Samson said to the lad who held him by the hand, "Let me feel the pillars which support the temple, so that I can lean on them." Now the temple was full of men and women. All the lords of the Philistines were there—about three thousand men and women on the roof watching while Samson performed.

Then Samson called to the LORD, saying, "O Lord GOD, remember me, I pray! Strengthen me, I pray, just this once, O God, that I may with one blow take vengeance on the Philistines for my two eyes!" And Samson took hold of the two middle pillars which supported the temple, and he braced himself against them, one on his right and the other on his left. Then Samson said, "Let me die with the Philistines!" And he pushed with all his might, and the temple fell on the lords and all the people who were in it. So the dead that he killed at his death were more than he had killed in his life (Judges 16:25-30).

No tumbled columns, collapsed Bronze Age temples, or ill-placed gates have been found in Gaza yet.[8] There are no well-funded, university-led archaeological expeditions to the area, and any artifacts that have been uncovered (too often by bulldozers) find their way onto the black market or are stored by history-loving Palestinians who hope for a day when they can be properly studied and displayed.[9] Archaeologists can't even get the excavating tools they need through Israeli security and into Gaza for fear that militants would turn them into weapons.[10]

Gaza in the Palestinian National Authority (PNA)

The closest I've ever come to Gaza City was in 2004. Five volunteers from the Ashkelon dig rented a car to go tour some archaeological sites in the Negev. We were barely outside Ashkelon's city limits when we made a wrong turn and found ourselves approaching a heavily militarized crossing between Israel and the Palestinian territory called the Gaza Strip. Needless to say, we turned around and got out of the area as quickly as possible. There was no time for photographs.

Up until 2007, Gaza and the West Bank (the Palestinians' larger territory, which we will visit in chapter 8) were run by the Palestinian Authority, an elected governing body that had broad support from the international community and showed interest in preserving the area's long and rich history. But the new government, controlled by Hamas, is not so sensitive to the past. They have repeatedly leveled tels in favor of new construction.[11] Gaza is rich in archaeological artifacts, but poor in livable space. Over 1.8 million people live in an area that is only 130 square miles; that's like taking the entire population of Phoenix and cramming everyone into one-quarter of the city limits.

In addition to being cramped and poverty-ridden, the Gaza Strip is physically and militarily blocked off from the rest of the world. Situated only 13 kilometers south of Ashkelon, Gazan rockets can (and frequently do) hit the Israeli city, but its citizens cannot easily go to Ashkelon themselves to shop, work, vacation, or worship. And almost every day, angry militants cause and respond to military conflict with Israel.

In a series of three tweets in 2019 citing two magazine articles,[12] Israeli Prime Minister Benjamin Netanyahu reminded the world that the word *Palestinian* is derived from the word *Philistine*, although the two groups are not ethnically related:

> A new study of DNA recovered from an ancient Philistine site in the Israeli city of Ashkelon confirms what we know from the Bible—that the origin of the Philistines is in southern Europe. The Bible mentions a place called Caphtor, which is probably modern-day Crete. *There's no connection between the ancient Philistines & the modern Palestinians, whose ancestors came from the Arabian Peninsula to the Land of Israel thousands of years later. The Palestinians' connection to the Land of Israel is nothing compared to the 4,000-year connection that the Jewish people have with the land.*[13]

In those last two sentences, the prime minister both admits that modern Palestinians are not related to ancient Philistines and uses the European DNA of the unrelated ancient Philistines as an opportunity to nullify modern Palestinian claims on the land. The region of Palestine was given its name nearly 2,000 years ago by the Roman occupiers, but the people living there neither then nor now were genetically related to the ancient Philistines.

The backstory for this tweet was that, in 2016, the last excavation team at Ashkelon uncovered a Philistine cemetery. There was enough DNA in the bones for experts to be able to test where the Philistines came from. Up until that point everyone had assumed, based on material culture, that the Sea Peoples were from some islands in the Mediterranean. Their pottery art and forms were similar to Aegean forms, but there had been no irrefutable proof that the Sea Peoples came from the Mediterranean. Pottery forms could have been borrowed or copied, some might have argued, but DNA evidence in human bones is hard evidence.

Only days before I landed in Israel, two of my Ashkelon and Shimron acquaintances, Daniel Master and Adam Aja, published their findings along with several of their colleagues.[14] They expected (and deserved!) a celebratory moment from historians around the world for solving one of the great mysteries of the Bible. Instead, they got pulled into the politics of the Palestinian-Israeli conflict simply because a current group of people—with zero connection to the ancients my friends wrote about—happened to sort of share a name with their ancient subjects. The statement by Netanyahu is confusing because, as he himself admits, there is no connection between the past and the present.

MEANWHILE, BACK AT TEL ASHKELON...

As if to announce divine displeasure to the group of tourists looking intensely at the little sign representing an old "golden" calf, we hear a sonic boom and become keenly aware of the mere 13 kilometers between us and the Gaza Strip.

It is almost noon, and the Israeli forces are practicing maneuvers and breaking the sound barrier over the Mediterranean. There are several planes in formation above our heads, but there is nothing to worry about this time. No rockets are coming our way from Gaza.

An expatriate Ethiopian living in Israel points up at the sky. "Thank you, thank you," he says to me in heavily accented English. Because it is obvious that I have no idea what he is talking about, he continues to point at the planes: "America. Thank you, thank you, America." After a solid minute of this, I realize he is crediting my country with protecting his. We gave Israel those planes.

CHAPTER 3

DEATH AND LIFE IN NEGEV'S DUSTY DESERT

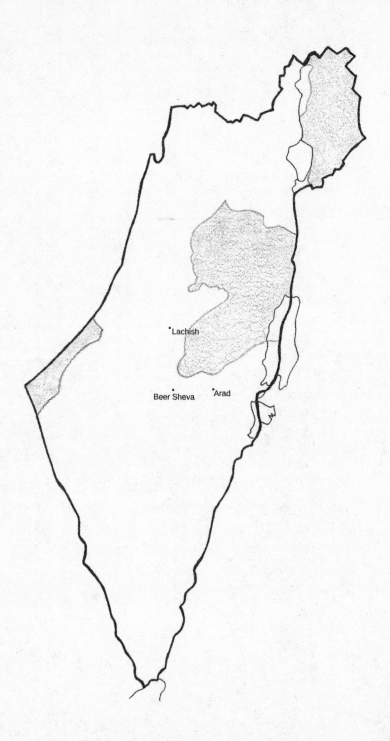

Probably most famous as the place where Moses and the Hebrews wandered for a generation, the Negev is a desert region in Israel that covers roughly the southern half of the country. The word *Negev* doesn't appear in the Bible, but other geographical indicators in the biblical text leave little doubt it is where the Israelite religion had its formal beginning. In the desert, God gave His Law to Moses and the Hebrews (Exodus 20–23), the first sacrifices took place (Exodus 24:1-11), the ark of the covenant and its tabernacle were constructed (Exodus 25–27), and all the priests were ordained (Exodus 28–29).

Geologically speaking, a *desert* is defined as "arid land with usually sparse vegetation; especially, such land having a very warm climate and receiving less than 25 centimeters (10 inches) of sporadic rainfall annually."[1] With rainfall amounts between 10 and 20 centimeters each year, the southern half of Israel falls easily into the category.[2] Based on these numbers alone, it is not surprising that the Hebrews were longing for God's promised "land flowing with milk and honey" (Exodus 13:5). They had left the region of the Nile Delta, which was lush and green thanks to the river and irrigation, and they were wandering around in dry dust.

Just to the west of the Negev, in the coastal plains where our Philistine friends flourished, increasing efforts in irrigation and farming have given the Israeli government a reputation for "making the desert bloom." Thanks to well-coordinated human efforts during the last 100 years, the Negev has been slowly shrinking instead of expanding.[3]

KIBBUTZ OR MOSHAV?

Not many people realize that modern Israel started out as a socialist nation and still retains some socialist systems today. In the late 1800s and early 1900s, wealthy European and Russian Jews began buying large swaths of land within British Mandated Palestine. As Jews were facing increasing persecution in Europe and Asia, they began moving to Palestine and settling in communes on those properties where the citizens agreed to share property equally and were agriculturally self-sufficient. No one "owned" anything on a *kibbutz*, and no one was homeless. This practice continues today, and the farming and irrigation efforts of the *kibbutzim* feed Israel.

As some kibbutzim began to have surpluses of goods and citizens became more acquainted with capitalism, the idea of the *moshav* developed. When the *moshavim* are initially set up by the government, slivers of land are granted to settlers and all jobs are assigned, but citizens are allowed to own property and sell their goods. This system works by taxing the citizens immensely. According to one of our tour guides, citizens "give" over 75 percent of their income to the moshav leaders, who then distribute money and services (such as health care) equally among everyone who works there.

WAR, WORSHIP, AND WATER

Most of the cities in the Negev don't have detailed histories in the Bible. Places such as Arad tend to pop up in the text when invaders are sweeping through an area, and they are conquered and abandoned

When I picture a desert, I imagine grains of sand and cacti. But in the Negev, the terrain is layers of dry dirt punctuated by the occasional scrubby-brush bush.

within a verse or two (Joshua 12:14). (Beer Sheva is the obvious exception.) This isn't terribly surprising since most of the Negev's ancient population (and some of its current population) were nomadic Bedouins. Many settlements were impermanent because the people moved around so much. Rarely were stone or brick structures built that would last for generations, although the ones that were built are worth visiting today.

BEDOUIN CULTURE

Historically, the Arab-Muslim Bedouin tribes roamed the southern Negev region of Israel as they raised livestock. In 1858, the Ottoman Empire passed the Land Law aimed at controlling the Bedouins' movement, registering land ownership, and increasing the tax base. All landowners were to notify the state of their holdings; any land not claimed was considered to be the property of the state.

When Israel came to power in 1948, the new nation continued the Ottomans' plan of forcibly settling the Bedouin people. Over time, the majority of nomadic Bedouins became semi-nomadic and eventually settled. Today's Bedouin townships in Israel may be likened to Native American tribal reservations in the United States. The state designated an area, built an infrastructure, and then insisted the transient people settle permanently in those areas.[4]

Tel Arad

Halfway between Beer Sheva and the Dead Sea is the ancient city of Arad. Excavations tell us that it was probably founded around the time the Hebrews were wandering in the area, and it was continuously occupied until Nebuchadnezzar conquered it and the rest of Judah in 586 BCE.[5]

The Bible mentions Arad as a landmark a few times, but it actually describes the conquest of its Canaanite citizens by the Israelites:

> The king of Arad, the Canaanite, who dwelt in the South, heard that Israel was coming on the road to Atharim. Then he fought against Israel and took some of them prisoners. So Israel made a vow to the LORD, and said, "If You will indeed deliver this people into my hand, then I will utterly destroy their cities." And the LORD listened to the voice of Israel and delivered up the Canaanites, and they utterly destroyed them and their cities. So the name of that place was called Hormah (Numbers 21:1-3).

There wasn't much there for Joshua and Caleb to attack in the Late Bronze Age—just an unwalled village on top of a mound—but as soon as David and Solomon took over Israel at the beginning of the Iron Age, Arad became a fortified city whose defenses and public buildings seem to have been under constant renovation and expansion. Sometimes that work resulted from a war. For example, Egyptian pharaoh

Shishak destroyed two fortresses called Arad, according to his victory relief at Karnak.[6]

The Israelites gave Arad major upgrades after Shishak burned through the city. They built walls that were up to 12 feet thick, and they centered their new gateway on the eastern wall of the city, flanked by massive towers. At the same time, they seem to have enlarged their worship space and created a "holy of holies" according to the Exodus requirements: The altar stones were unhewn (20:25) and measured "five cubits long and five cubits wide" (27:1).[7]

Before Solomon's temple was finished, Israelites were allowed to worship God in remote "high places," but as soon as the ark of the covenant was settled in Jerusalem's holy of holies, those high places were supposed to be closed down. So why would Israelites living in a Judahite city (belonging to the tribe of Judah and within the Southern Kingdom) choose to build a temple when Solomon's temple was where Israelites were actively and properly worshiping Him in Jerusalem? I suggest it was for two reasons: tradition and laziness. Archaeology reveals that prior to Shishak's attack and prior to Solomon's temple, the people of Arad had worshiped from that exact location. They built

Arad is most famous as the first place a holy of holies was discovered in Israel.

their new-and-improved temple over the remains of the previous one and just kept worshiping from there. They probably thought it kept them from wasting the time it took to travel back and forth to Jerusalem, about 50 miles each way. When we get to Beer Sheva, we will learn that God didn't approve of this disobedience.

Tel Lachish

I had my first I-can't-believe-I'm-standing-here moment of the trip as I was approaching Tel Lachish. It doesn't get a whole lot of press in the Bible—it is best known as the city from which the Assyrian Sennacherib organized his siege of Jerusalem (2 Kings 18–19)—but this city's excavation has been vital to understanding how Israel's history fits with that of its neighbors.

During the Late Bronze Age, Lachish was a booming city-state whose Canaanite residents traded with Egypt. Letters between the leaders have been found in Egypt's official records from the fourteenth century BCE. Iron Age Judahite Lachish is mentioned in two panels from a wall relief in Sennacherib's Assyrian palace and in his prism-shaped official Assyrian court records. (Sennacherib was obviously quite proud of his conquest of Lachish.) Such extrabiblical records seem to corroborate the Bible's stories, as do destruction layers in the soil.

In the Bible, the city of Lachish has two memorable moments. In Joshua 10, Joshua hangs their king from a tree and then takes the city from the Canaanites. The other is recorded in 2 Kings 18–19 when the Assyrian emperor Sennacherib commands his army from Lachish while negotiating a steep tribute from Jerusalem.

> Then Joshua passed from Libnah, and all Israel with him, to Lachish; and they encamped against it and fought against it. And the LORD delivered Lachish into the hand of Israel, who took it on the second day, and struck it and all the people who were in it with the edge of the sword, according to all that he had done to Libnah. Then Horam king of Gezer came up to help Lachish; and Joshua struck him and his people, until he left him none remaining.

From Lachish Joshua passed to Eglon, and all Israel with him; and they encamped against it and fought against it. They took it on that day and struck it with the edge of the sword; all the people who were in it he utterly destroyed that day, according to all that he had done to Lachish (Joshua 10:31-35).

And in the fourteenth year of King Hezekiah, Sennacherib king of Assyria came up against all the fortified cities of Judah and took them. Then Hezekiah king of Judah sent to the king of Assyria at Lachish, saying, "I have done wrong; turn away from me; whatever you impose on me I will pay." And the king of Assyria assessed Hezekiah king of Judah 300 talents of silver and 30 talents of gold. So Hezekiah gave him all the silver that was found in the house of the LORD and in the treasuries of the king's house. At that time Hezekiah stripped the gold from the doors of the temple of the LORD, and from the pillars which Hezekiah king of Judah had overlaid, and gave it to the king of Assyria (2 Kings 18:13-16).

View finders all over the tel show visitors what the city's palace would have looked like almost three thousand years ago.

Lachish's reputation as a military power is well deserved, as archaeological excavations and restorations demonstrate. After Jerusalem, Lachish was the second-most-important city in the region. Situated about 25 miles southwest of Judah's capital near the border of the Northern and Southern Kingdoms, Lachish was massively fortified to defend against Judah's enemies (first the Philistines and Egyptians, and later the Assyrians and Babylonians). The Iron Age walls were six meters thick, and they were built upon a *glacis* (a massive slope that keeps invaders from scaling the walls or tunneling under them) that was surrounded by a dry moat. There was only one gate for accessing the city. Within the city walls, the palace and other administrative buildings were on top of the tel and in the center of the city (where the breezes and views were best for the wealthiest citizens!). Around that governing center, many houses were built haphazardly.[8]

Archaeological work at Tel Lachish continues. As an official Israeli park, it is preserved, maintained, and improved by the state, but the

History and modernity coexist in this place. Tel Lachish sits among many active, irrigated farms that feed Israel's citizens while visitors learn about the starvation that occurred within Lachish's walls during sieges.

Israel Antiquities Authority has authorized professors from Hebrew University and the Austrian Academy of Sciences to continue excavating the remains of a Middle Bronze Age palace.[9] It was one of the best sites that we visited, full of informational panels, iron artwork, easy paths, and even Bible quotations.

Tel Beer Sheva

In Genesis 21, the Bible tells us how the city of Beer Sheva (also transliterated *Beersheba* in some Bible translations) got its well, and how that well got its name:

> So Abraham rose early in the morning, and took bread and a skin of water; and putting it on her shoulder, he gave it and the boy to Hagar, and sent her away. Then she departed and wandered in the Wilderness of Beersheba. And the water in the skin was used up, and she placed the boy under one of the shrubs. Then she went and sat down across from him at a distance of about a bowshot; for she said to herself, "Let me not see the death of the boy." So she sat opposite him, and lifted her voice and wept.
>
> And God heard the voice of the lad. Then the angel of God called to Hagar out of heaven, and said to her, "What ails you, Hagar? Fear not, for God has heard the voice of the lad where he is. Arise, lift up the lad and hold him with your hand, for I will make him a great nation."
>
> Then God opened her eyes, and she saw a well of water. And she went and filled the skin with water, and gave the lad a drink (Genesis 21:14-19).
>
> Then Abraham rebuked Abimelech because of a well of water which Abimelech's servants had seized. And Abimelech said, "I do not know who has done this thing; you did not tell me, nor had I heard of it until today." So Abraham took sheep and oxen and gave them to Abimelech, and the two of them made a covenant. And Abraham set seven ewe lambs of the flock by themselves.

> Then Abimelech asked Abraham, "What is the meaning of these seven ewe lambs which you have set by themselves?"
>
> And he said, "You will take these seven ewe lambs from my hand, that they may be my witness that I have dug this well." Therefore he called that place Beersheba, because the two of them swore an oath there (Genesis 21:25-31).

A heavenly messenger taps the well for Hagar and Ishmael (who happens to be a 17-year-old man at this point in the story, so don't go picturing an infant under that shrub brush!). According to the text so far, no human hands were involved in the digging of that well.

When the water source is later discovered by Abimelech's men, he tries to take ownership of it. This is not surprising; as geology and Scripture attest, water is scarce in the Negev. But Abraham's response to this is curious. He (presumably) lies to Abimelech when he claims that his men dug the well (because we just learned that a heavenly messenger did it), but then he doesn't stick to his guns. He goes ahead and "pays" Abimelech for the well by gifting him seven ewe lambs after making a treaty with the Canaanite king.

A few chapters later, Genesis gives a second origin story for Beer Sheva, this one starring Abraham's son Isaac but with a lot of similarities to his father's account. One big difference: Isaac built an altar there. He and his descendants lived there and worshiped God from there until joining his grandson, Joseph, in Egypt (Genesis 46).

> Then [Isaac] went up from there to Beersheba. And the LORD appeared to him the same night and said, "I am the God of your father Abraham; do not fear, for I am with you. I will bless you and multiply your descendants for My servant Abraham's sake." So he built an altar there and called on the name of the LORD, and he pitched his tent there; and there Isaac's servants dug a well.
>
> Then Abimelech came to him from Gerar with Ahuzzath, one of his friends, and Phichol the commander of his army. And Isaac said to them, "Why have you come to me, since you hate me and have sent me away from you?"

But they said, "We have certainly seen that the LORD is with you. So we said, 'Let there now be an oath between us, between you and us; and let us make a covenant with you, that you will do us no harm, since we have not touched you, and since we have done nothing to you but good and have sent you away in peace. You are now the blessed of the LORD.'"

So he made them a feast, and they ate and drank. Then they arose early in the morning and swore an oath with one another; and Isaac sent them away, and they departed from him in peace.

It came to pass the same day that Isaac's servants came and told him about the well which they had dug, and said to him, "We have found water." So he called it Shebah. Therefore the name of the city is Beersheba to this day (Genesis 26:23-33).

In this case, Isaac's servants did actually dig the well. But I'm more interested in that altar.

Before Solomon's temple was finished, and certainly before God's rules of religion were handed down to the Hebrews at Mount Sinai, altars were all over biblical Israel. They were seemingly lawfully erected by Noah, Abra(ha)m, Isaac, Jacob, Moses, Aaron, and Joshua. During those men's lifetimes, God was yet to settle into His temple and declare Jerusalem as the only place His people could worship Him by making sacrifices.

But something changes near the end of the book of Joshua when "the children of Reuben, the children of Gad, and half the tribe of Manasseh built an altar there by the Jordan—a great, impressive altar" (Joshua 22:10). The rest of the Israelite tribes storm the builders to ask them, "What treachery is this that you have committed against the God of Israel, to turn away this day from following the LORD, in that you have built for yourselves an altar, that you might rebel this day against the LORD?" (Joshua 22:16). When the three tribes explain that the altar is to be a remembrance—so their future generations will feel connected to the other Israelite tribes who live across the Jordan River and continue to worship their God—the rest of Israel cools off and decides their "remembrance altar" is okay so long as it is never actually used.

Why would one altar, erected by God's people to remember and/or worship Him, be problematic when similar altars were in use across the Israelite territory? Scholars have suggested several potential answers to this question:

1. God did not direct the building of the altar; therefore, it was illegitimate.

2. The area where it was built, west of the Jordan River, was not considered part of God's promised land by the other tribes.

3. As the Israelite tribes were settling, God wanted centralized worship so He would be distinguished from the Canaanite gods.[10]

Ironically, the problem implicit in answer number two—that the West Jordan tribes were separated from the East Jordan tribes—is

Thanks to the Israel Parks Authority and UNESCO, it is easy to walk among the partially reconstructed buildings of Tel Beer Sheva and imagine yourself living in one of the houses that backs up to the city wall, working in the administrative center, and "holding court" with the city elders inside the gate's chambers.

exactly why the altar was built. The West Jordan tribes did fear that they would become separated from the rest of the Israelites and God Himself because their descendants would live in closer proximity to their Canaanite neighbors than their Israelite brothers and sisters. What they and all of the Israelites really needed was a central temple where everyone came to sacrifice to God. Then all tribes would be linked by tradition, faith, and pilgrimage.

After the ark and the tabernacle were made but before Solomon finished his temple, the presence of altars in places other than Jerusalem was confusing for the Israelites. The story in Joshua makes it clear they were less than ideal and a subject of intense debate, but they weren't exactly illegal yet because there was no centralized place of worship for everyone. However, once the temple was built, the ark of the covenant was in the holy of holies, and God resided over His seat there, the altars were nothing but potential troublemakers.

Throughout most of 1 and 2 Kings, the Israelites of both the Northern and Southern Kingdoms continue to worship God in places other than Jerusalem and in ways He does not sanction. The northern tribes might deserve a bit more human understanding here: They were politically shut off from their temple in Jerusalem after Solomon's death and civil war split Israel into the two kingdoms. None of their citizens could physically travel to Jerusalem, so they had two "high places" instead at Dan and Bethel. In those sanctuaries, they worshiped not only God but some of their foreign neighbors' deities, such as Ba'al and Asherah.

In the Southern Kingdom, in spite of their proximity to Jerusalem and prophets' warnings against it, the Judahites also created their own local "high places." One of those was at Tel Beer Sheva. But a few kings, such as Hezekiah, set out to destroy the shrines (2 Kings 18:1-4). In 2 Kings 22–23, King Josiah finds the Book of the Law and returns Judah's people to the right and proper worship of God:

> Then the king stood by a pillar and made a covenant before
> the LORD, to follow the LORD and to keep His command-
> ments and His testimonies and His statutes, with all his

heart and all his soul, to perform the words of this covenant that were written in this book. And all the people took a stand for the covenant. And the king commanded Hilkiah the high priest, the priests of the second order, and the door-keepers, to bring out of the temple of the LORD all the articles that were made for Baal, for Asherah, and for all the host of heaven; and he burned them outside Jerusalem in the fields of Kidron, and carried their ashes to Bethel…And he brought all the priests from the cities of Judah, and defiled the high places where the priests had burned incense, from Geba to Beersheba; also he broke down the high places at the gates which were at the entrance of the Gate of Joshua the governor of the city, which were to the left of the city gate (2 Kings 23:3-8).

After reading Genesis's naming stories for Beer Sheva and learning just how troublesome non-temple altars could be, it is hardly surprising that excavated and reconstructed Tel Beer Sheva is most famous for two things from the time of Israel's kings: a giant, two-source water system and a four-horned altar.

When archaeological sites are restored in Israel, the experts want visitors to discern between what was there in antiquity, and what has been added back. They will install a clay line (which I have highlighted here) indicating the original existing stones are below it, and the re-created structure is above it.

At Tel Beer Sheva stands a reconstruction of a four-horned altar that was once used in the city. When archaeologists discovered it, the altar had been knocked over and the horns broken off. Many scholars argue this is evidence of King Josiah's desecration of the illegal high places throughout Judah.

Throughout the Iron Age (1200 BCE–586 BCE), the city at Tel Beer Sheva was occupied and active. It was at its largest and strongest just before it was attacked and destroyed by Sennacherib in 701 BCE, as was its neighboring fortress city, Lachish. Beer Sheva also had great walls, many large houses, an administrative palace, and storerooms.

Its water system was most impressive. The actual well at Beer Sheva, which produced the water that the city used on ordinary days, was outside of the city's defenses. In the ninth century, the city planners had the idea to build a giant cistern below the city and within its walls so that the citizens would have access to water in the event that a siege would trap them all inside. A reservoir that would hold 700 cubic meters was carved out of the ground's chalk rock and then plastered to keep the water from leeching back into the ground. A feeder channel would then direct seasonal floodwaters from nearby streams into the reservoir, and citizens would access the underground water by climbing down a 17-meter-deep shaft lined with rock and a spiral staircase.[11]

Prior to cultic reforms by Josiah or Hezekiah, Beer Sheva apparently had its own shrine, as did Tel Arad. In the 1970s, Yohanan Aharoni discovered the pieces of a 63-inch-tall-and-wide horned altar that had been dismantled and then reused when a newer wall was built.[12] This was the first altar for animal sacrifices to have been found in Israel, and it was significantly larger than all other altars. For reference, I am 63 inches tall, and a queen-sized bed is 60 inches across: I would fit perfectly on this altar as long as someone gave me a boost to get up on it!

To see the original altar pieces, you must go to the Israel Museum in Jerusalem. A replica is displayed near the visitor's center as you enter and exit Tel Beer Sheva.

TEL SHEVA

While we were touring Beer Sheva, I noticed that my active, history-loving father was really slowing down. He is the one person I can always count on to "geek out" with me and read every single panel at every single site or museum.

The four of us had been in direct sun for several hours when we finally climbed up into a covered observation tower at the site. Breathing heavily, my dad announced that he wasn't feeling well and that he wanted to return to the car to rest. In spite of my obnoxious, constant reminders that everyone (myself included) drink water and electrolytes, we noticed that his water bottle was practically full.

"Ross, why aren't you drinking your water?" David asked.

"Because I'm not sweating," he answered.

I was recently acquainted with the symptoms of dehydration and heatstroke. For most of my time at Shimron, the temperature stayed below 100 degrees. But one day we were struck by a fast-moving front that brought extreme heat, high winds, and much dust from the Saudi Arabian desert. We had been warned that the temperature would climb to 104 that day between 11:00 a.m. and 3:00 p.m., and we were constantly reminded to drink water.

As the winds blew in, I began to get a little headache, and then became very nauseated. A microbiologist who was taking samples in our

The walk through Beer Sheva's ninth-century cistern is the highlight of the site's tour. After descending the modern wooden stairs alongside the shaft's ancient curving staircase and wandering around the cool reservoir, guests exit the cistern here and reenter the blinding sunlight.

square saw me getting wobbly, and he told me in his thick South African accent, "These are the khamsin winds." I didn't quite understand him at that moment, but I heard enough to think, *If these winds have a name, then they must be brutal.* I was right. In spite of drinking 24 ounces of water each hour of the day and adding electrolyte tablets, I had to cut my workday short and head back to the dorms or risk heatstroke.

It took every ounce of strength I had to walk back to the cars as the burning wind crossed the tel. The Jezreel Valley to my right looked more like smog-filled Los Angeles as the dusty air contaminated lungs and shortened visibility; the Carmel mountains were totally obscured. As I approached the compound, I almost literally ran into the dig director, who is also fair-skinned and dehydration-prone. "I just can't drink enough water today, can you?" It was hyperbole on his part, but for me, the answer was no.

That day on the tel, I learned how dehydration progesses to heatstroke. First you stop urinating, then you stop sweating. You get a headache, and then your stomach gets upset. My father was experiencing all those symptoms, and if I didn't get him an Oral Rehydration Solution quickly, then I'd be driving him to a hospital for an IV bag.

I searched my phone for the nearest pharmacy, assuming they would carry an ORS. Thankfully, there was one less than a mile away in a Bedouin township called Tel Sheva (or Tel as-Sabi, as transliterated from Arabic). Following the GPS, I drove into the town and noticed lots of giant *square* speed bumps and constant roundabouts. Many of the buildings were made from old shipping containers, and men started walking out of them and following us on foot. The place seemed to have been designed to keep outsiders out, and wow, was I an outsider: a woman piloting a vehicle—with her bright-red hair uncovered—while two men sat in "lesser" positions in the car.

I quickly realized I wasn't going to find a pharmacy there as I turned into a little dead-end neighborhood. When a man looked me in the eyes and adjusted a very large gun, I hightailed it out of there. Voices from the passenger seats cheered me on, "Drive, drive, drive!" until I got to those speed bumps, and they switched to, "Don't damage the rental car!" and "Ouch! Slow down!"

After that adventure, my dad decided he could skip the pharmacy, and I loaded him down with electrolyte tablets. It took him three days to recover.

WATER IS LIFE

All over Israel, and especially in the Negev, water was and is synonymous with life. Cities initially popped up around water sources, and those same cities were the first to be fortified against foreigners wanting to steal their water supplies. Engineering marvels such as the cistern at Beer Sheva are unmistakable, physical reminders of this truth. Rare and precious water was used in purification rituals of all religions, just as Christians are baptized today.

Water is still quite the commodity in Israel. What makes the western side of the Negev bloom today, thanks to human efforts in irrigation and farming, just might be "killing" the natural resource that marks the desert's eastern boundary: the Dead Sea.

CHAPTER 4

BOBBING IN WATER AND HIKING TO CAVES AT THE DEAD SEA

I t's been fifteen years since you've seen the Dead Sea?" my grid supervisor and former Harvard buddy asked me. "You won't recognize it."

In 2004, I had visited the Dead Sea with some dig friends just long enough to experience the heavy feeling of being below sea level, to bob in the slippery hot water, and to giggle at the nearly nude sunbathers covered in the rich, black, Dead Sea mud. The beach was made of salt—not sand—and the sharp crystals would slice the bottoms of your feet if you weren't wearing shoes.

When I returned to the Dead Sea in 2019 with my husband and parents, the situation was different. Israel had invested a lot of money in building up resort areas with many huge hotels, beach services such as permanent umbrellas and showers, and a layer of sand covering the spikey shards of salt on the shore. The famous Dead Sea mud must have been somewhere under that sand, too, but we never saw any. Tourism is big business at the Dead Sea, and it seemed that investors were trying to make a visit there more like a visit to the Mediterranean.

I wonder if they are trying to make money while they can, because the Dead Sea is "dying": "This one-of-a-kind sea is receding at an alarming rate…Back in the 1960s, the shoreline was almost up to the road. Now, in some areas, it's a mile away. And as the water declines, the beach

While we bobbed, other visitors covered themselves in the black mud. Many would sit on the coastline for hours letting the sun bake the rich minerals into their skin. We were told that it has a healing effect on psoriasis and eczema, and the thick air is good for asthmatics.

has become inundated with sinkholes—six thousand and counting."[1] Many areas around the coast now look like a war zone as buildings have been abandoned and roads are crumbling into the sinkholes.

In the past, the Jordan River transferred a constant amount of fresh water from the Sea of Galilee to the Dead Sea. But as Israel's population grew and national agricultural projects such as the kibbutzim required more water than God gave them, the government built the National Water Carrier that diverts millions of gallons of water to the Negev desert and the Mediterranean coast and away from the Sea of Galilee. Farther upstream, Syria dammed the headwaters that should feed the Sea of Galilee, further reducing how much water could make it into the Jordan and down to the Dead Sea. Today, over 96 percent of the water that used to go into the Dead Sea no longer reaches it. And because Israel and Jordan are mining the southern part of the sea for potash and other minerals and chemicals, what water does enter the sea is intentionally evaporated more quickly by industry.[2]

A team of scientists and politicians from Israel, Palestine, and Jordan have developed a plan to save the Dead Sea while also getting more drinking water to desert areas of Palestine and Jordan. The ten-billion-dollar Red Sea–Dead Sea Conveyance Project will put a desalination plant on the shores of the Red Sea. The country of Jordan will get the fresh water their growing population so desperately needs, while the brine that is a by-product of the desalination process will be dumped into the Dead Sea by a large, long pipeline.

But this is an experiment, and it might not work. The Dead Sea and Red Sea have never been connected in human history. In Beer Sheva, scientists are testing how the brine might affect the Dead Sea's ecosystem. When the waters meet in the lab, they form gypsum (like that powdery stuff in drywall) that could turn the Dead Sea white. In the real world—the Great Salt Lake to be precise—introduction of a low-saline brine has increased the algae and turned the lake red. (So the Red Sea–Dead Sea Project could turn the Dead Sea red!) If the plan goes forward, scientists will start releasing brine in stages. If nothing goes wrong, they will continue to up the amount until they are emptying 200 billion gallons of Red Sea brine into the Dead Sea each year.[3]

In what might be a silver lining to this tragic story of the Dead Sea's slow death by human interference in natural water flow, the cooperation required between Israelis, Palestinians, and Jordanians to pull off the Red Sea–Dead Sea project could help lessen overall political tensions in their region. The State of Israel, which tends to receive most of the blame for the shrinking Dead Sea and for water shortages in Jordan and Palestine, has already directed more of the Sea of Galilee's water to the other two areas to quench their populations' thirst. Israel has also pioneered desalination, finding ways to make it easier and more afford-able, and they are applying that technology to the project. One can only hope that the nations can learn to be thankful for each other as they work together to save an important natural resource and hydrate all people in the region.[4]

MASADA

A few months before I left for Israel, David and I were poking around a used bookstore to find some business and architecture titles for a new bookcase in his office. Architecture and Archaeology are not far apart there, so I got a little distracted and found a gem of my own: a first American edition of *Masada: Herod's Fortress and the Zealots' Last Stand.*[5] The dust jacket is pretty beat up, but the pages inside haven't yellowed at all. The book was released in 1966 at the same time that Israel opened up the site to tourists. It tells the stories of the people who lived and died there in the first century and of the excavations that took place between 1953 and 1965.

Masada sits on top of a high plateau overlooking the Dead Sea. Construction of what would become Herod the Great's winter palace began after the Maccabean Revolt (when the Jews retook control of their region from the Roman Empire) during the first century BCE. It began as a small fortress, but Herod supervised the building of an entire city, including multiple palaces and residences, cisterns, storehouses, hot and cold baths, and stables all within a formidable casemate wall. As the Romans regained control of Judea, it became a garrison for Roman troops between 6 CE and 66 CE.

In 66 CE, at the beginning of the Jews' Great Revolt against Rome, a group of Jewish rebels took Masada back and began living there. As

Looking down from the northern palace's upper terrace, where Herod would have slept.

the Jews were losing their war for control of Judea and especially after the fall of the temple in 70 CE, other Jews fled to Masada, forming what would be the last rebel stronghold.

WINTER AT MASADA

If you visit Masada during the summer, as most guests do, you'll find yourself wondering how people could have survived there—and why they would have wanted to survive there! The city is very difficult to access, the sun is unbearable after 10 a.m., and the only water in sight is 37 percent salt.

Life in that region depended on the winter rains and engineering. Herod built a complete water system that managed to put Tel Beer Sheva's to shame! Dams diverted winter floods from neighboring slopes into channels that directed the water into 12 rock-hewn cisterns below the city. Pack animals would bring the water up through the city gates and pour it into the "plumbing" that supplied water not only for drinking but also for elaborate Roman baths. Renewed excavations since 2017 have revealed that Masada did not lack in water. Agricultural remains prove the city was filled with gardens and even supported a vineyard.[6] Herod made his own oasis in the desert.

According to the historian Josephus, the Romans besieged Masada for several months in 73 CE. Just before they broke through the city walls, the leader of the rebel city convinced the men that it would be better to commit suicide than be captured by the Romans. The men agreed to kill their own wives and children; and then they wrote their names on pottery sherds, tossed them into a container, and drew out ten names. Those ten men murdered all the other men, then drew lots again, leaving one man to kill the other nine and then commit suicide. When the Romans broke through, they found the human carnage

Mosaics in the bath house.

along with two women and five children who had hidden in a cistern and told them the story.

The Romans occupied the site for about 30 years before abandoning it entirely. About 300 years later, during the Byzantine period, a monastery was founded on the plateau and survived until the rise of Islam in the seventh century CE. Masada then sat empty for 1,200 years until it was rediscovered by scholars in the late nineteenth century.

Today, Masada is the most-visited park in Israel, and its amenities reflect that fact. As you approach Masada from the main road down next to the Dead Sea, you first see a massive visitor's center carved out of the side of a cliff. It contains an underground parking garage, a small theater, two museums, a food-court-style cafeteria, and a giant gift shop that specializes in Dead Sea beauty products. After buying your tickets there and looking around for a bit, it is easy to forget that the main attraction is still far above your head on top of that cliff.

There are tons of tour companies that will charge you lots of money to tell you all about Masada, but you really don't need more than what the Parks Authority provides with your ticket. Their two-hour-long audio tour is available to borrow using a government-issued ID as collateral. You'll want to be there early—it gets very hot, very quickly up there with very little shade—and take a hat and water bottle. Masada, along with most other national sites, provides drinking fountains. But don't worry—it comes from modern plumbing, not the two-millennia-old cisterns!

CASTING LOTS

At Jesus's crucifixion, all four Gospels describe the Roman soldiers "casting lots" for His garments. As I read these verses growing up, I imagined two soldiers squatting at the foot of the cross and throwing dice in a winner-takes-all kind of game. Although dice did exist in the first-century Roman Empire, that is not what our Bibles are describing.

Based on archaeological finds, it is more likely that the Roman soldiers were "casting lots" the same way that the Israelites and Jews did throughout their history. Men would write their names on a pottery sherd (like those found at Masada) and then throw or "cast" it into a container. Someone would then draw out names. This is how corporate decisions were made, including which tribe got what land (Joshua 18:8), who got what job (1 Chronicles 25:8), and who would get thrown out of the boat (Jonah 1:7)!

The lots that were found at this spot in Masada were originally associated with Josephus's description of the mass suicide. Recently, some scholars have argued these may have simply been used by the city administrators for normal governance and that Josephus's story is more fable than fact.

WHAT IS A UNESCO WORLD HERITAGE SITE?

The United Nations Educational, Scientific and Cultural Organization (UNESCO) was formed in 1945 after the two world wars had destroyed many of the world's historical structures. In 1972, the first member states agreed to support UNESCO's World Heritage mission to identify, excavate, and preserve sites of cultural importance to local communities and all of humanity. Member states nominate sites within their borders that they want to save for future generations. A panel of experts evaluates the sites, and if they agree the sites should be protected and preserved, the members of the UNESCO World Heritage commission vote whether or not to accept the new sites.[7]

Including Masada, Israel and Palestine are currently home to 16 UNESCO World Heritage Sites, two of which are considered endangered: Battir (an agricultural region just southwest of Jerusalem) and the Old City of Hebron.

EN GEDI'S NATURE RESERVE

After about a week spent touring archaeological sites outside in the blistering heat, I was very excited to visit En Gedi. For the first time on this trip, we were going to do real hiking! I envisioned rushing rivers, lush vegetation, and a roaring waterfall keeping visitors—human and animal—cool in the middle of the desert.

Admittedly, I embellished the lushness of En Gedi as I described the area to my family (though we would later find abundant flora at Tel Dan). The water comes from two streams, which are mostly fed by the winter rains in the Judean hills. The En Gedi area is the largest oasis in Israel, but it has more rock than soil. There are no tree canopies to sit under, and the wildlife is limited. Historically, people have lived in cities adjacent to the oasis and used the water to irrigate crops planted in more fertile soil.[8] But life in and around En Gedi is becoming more dangerous as sinkholes are opening up: "As the sea declines, an underground layer of dry salt is left behind. Fresh water, like in winter flash floods, saturates that salt, which quickly dissolves, creating an underground cavity. Over time, it grows bigger, until, suddenly, without warning, the earth above it caves in."[9] The freshwater at En Gedi may be both its blessing and its curse as the ecology around the Dead Sea is changing.

It is easy to see why David (and the Jewish rebels a millennium later) would choose to hide in En Gedi. It is a rocky landscape full of caves and crevices where an entire army could easily hide while being sustained by the water, wildlife, and vegetation there. The strength and stability of the area may be waning today, but one can still see how it functioned as the setting for one peculiar Bible story. David has been anointed king of Israel by the prophet and judge Samuel, but King Saul sees David as a traitor and usurper. Saul is trying to capture David and

On the edge of the almost-dry riverbed, the Israel Nature and Parks Authority is working to keep animals from overgrazing on natural plants, so they protect some trees and grasses with cages. Rising high about the river is the natural "stronghold" where David may have camped.

keep his kingdom while also waging war against some of Israel's neighbors. While David and some of his men are hiding in the back of what must have been a pretty big cave, King Saul steps in to relieve himself. In such a vulnerable position, it would have been easy for David to kill Saul, but instead he uses his blade to take a swatch of fabric from Saul. This evidence of mercy, when later revealed to the king, causes him to agree that David will, indeed, be king of Israel one day—and a more righteous one than Saul could be (1 Samuel 23:29–24:22).

QUMRAN

About 20 miles north of En Gedi, an almost-identical version of David and Solomon's story was discovered in a cave at a site called Qumran. The Samuel Scroll, which is actually a collection of fragments containing bits of the biblical stories from 1 and 2 Samuel, was written in Hebrew by a group of ascetic Jews called the Essenes and has been dated between 50–25 BCE.

Around the same time that Herod was building Masada, the Essenes were living a communal life in and around the caves at Qumran. Their small village was built at the base of the cliffs and included functional communal rooms, such as an assembly hall, dining room, writing room (where the scrolls themselves were probably copied), stables, and ritual baths. The members themselves lived outside the buildings in huts and tents. As Herod did at Masada, the Essenes irrigated the city with aqueducts and stored water in cisterns. The constant flow of water was particularly important to this group because they took ritual purity seriously and bathed frequently.

In 68 CE, a few years before the conquest of Masada, the Romans conquered Qumran and evicted the Jews who lived there. The Essenes must have anticipated their coming demise because they hid the scrolls their group had been meticulously copying during the previous 200 years. In the cliffs above the Essene city, scrolls were hidden in jars and placed in caves where they would remain untouched for nearly 2,000 years. The area remained empty until 132 CE when the Romans returned and garrisoned men there. After the troops left in 135 CE, Qumran was forgotten.[10]

In 1947, Bedouin shepherds found seven scrolls in one of the caves at Qumran. Their find led to international excavations of the area and the discovery of thousands of scroll fragments and a few complete scrolls. The texts, which were well preserved thanks to the arid and salty air on the coast of the Dead Sea, contained all of the Old Testament (excepting Esther and Nehemiah), the Apocrypha, and many of the Essenes' own writings.

The discovery of the scrolls was dramatic, but that event might pale in comparison to the scrolls' road to publication. As of 1991, 44 years after their discovery, the Dead Sea Scrolls still had not been published. Herschel Shanks, the founder and long-time editor of *Biblical Archaeology Review* "went rogue" and printed the *Preliminary Edition of the Unpublished Dead Sea Scrolls—The Hebrew and Aramaic Texts from Cave Four.*[11] This action precipitated a groundswell of popular support leading to many foundations financially supporting the preservation of the scrolls and more research of them.[12]

Why are these old pieces of parchment, papyrus, and copper so important? Because prior to their discovery, the oldest manuscript we

The Samuel Scroll was among those found in Cave number 4, the first cave to be discovered.

had of the Hebrew Bible, called the Masoretic text, was from the ninth century CE. Some of the Dead Sea Scrolls are more than 1,000 years older than that. The Dead Sea Scrolls are almost word-for-word the same as the Masoretic text. In places where the Dead Sea Scrolls and the Masoretic text disagree, the Dead Sea Scrolls usually agree with the Septuagint. These similarities demonstrate that the Jews had, if not canonized, at least standardized their Scriptures before the destruction of their temple and diaspora of their people in 70 CE.[13]

HIKING TO THE CAVES

If you love hiking, consider climbing up to see some of the caves at Qumran that overlook the Essenes' city. After touring the ruins with my parents, David and I set off with our water bottles to climb to Cave 4, which is the closest to the ruins and happens to be where the first scrolls were found in 1947.

We couldn't quite make it into the cave—you really need proper climbing equipment to do that—but the effort was worth the view. We rested in a shady crevice for about half an hour looking out over the Dead Sea, thinking about the history surrounding us, and feeling close to God and the many generations of His people who had lived and died at this lowest place on earth.

ALONG THE WEST BANK

Highway 90 is the longest road in Israel, running from Eilat on the Red Sea to the Lebanese border and in between the Jordan River and the West Bank. It took us about two and a half hours of driving time to get from Masada to the Sea of Galilee, the next stop on our little adventure.

The road is owned and maintained by Israel, but technically, it is on the very eastern edge of the Palestinian West Bank. For this reason, it has a greater military presence than we had encountered so far. At large intersections, where Highway 90 intersects with roads heading toward Palestinian cities such as Jericho or Nablus, we noticed giant red signs that read in Hebrew, Arabic, and English, "This road leads to area 'A' under the Palestinian Authority. The entrance for Israeli citizens is forbidden, dangerous to your lives, and is against the Israeli law."

Israelis cannot cross into Palestine and vice versa. We knew this because we'd been unable to visit Gaza, and we would learn more about such travel restrictions when we would visit Hebron the next week. But driving along a straight road with the Dead Sea on the right and border fencing on the left, we asked ourselves what it would be like to be banned from visiting any part of the United States. As Americans, we freely travel between the states. We can go visit family members in Virginia, take a vacation in Hawaii, and worship at any place we'd like. Entering Canada and Mexico—any foreign country, really—is usually easy with an American passport. We never ask ourselves if we can go somewhere; we only have to decide when and how.

Conversation ended and the air got thick as we saw gates up ahead of us and cars slowing to a stop. On the boundary between the West Bank and the Israeli city of Beit Shean was a checkpoint. We knew we had nothing to worry about. All the drivers were stopping, saying a word or two to the crossing agent, and moving on. But then the van directly in front of us stopped and the conversation seemed to get heated. After searching the van, the agents let the vehicle go.

My mother was audibly nervous, and that forced me to act calmer than I felt. I told everyone to find their passports. I pulled forward, rolling down my window, and handed my passport to the twentysomething male guard. He looked at it with a furrowed brow, then told me to remove my sunglasses. Again and again, he looked at me and looked at my picture. Without another word, he handed it back and waved us into Israel.

CHAPTER 5

MEETING DISCIPLES AT THE SEA OF GALILEE

A few miles beyond the checkpoint at the West Bank–Israel border, the landscape changes dramatically. The dry grasses of the Negev desert give way to green as we enter a semiarid region of Israel: Galilee.

For the next few days, we have decided to make Tiberias our base. It is located on the western shore of the Sea of Galilee, about halfway up the coast, and after our last few days in the desert, we are thrilled to step out of the car into lake breezes and abundant flora. Tiberias sits in Lower Galilee, an area I found myself comparing to Colorado's front range. In Lower Galilee are several famous sites, including Nazareth and Megiddo, which we would visit in the coming days. About 25 miles north of Tiberias, we would exit the river valley and enter Upper Galilee, which is more mountainous and fertile.

Our first night there, my parents, David, and I walked from our hotel down to a seventeenth-century basalt building and had a lovely meal at Hermitage Oriental Restaurant. Surrounded by arched ceilings and stone walls, we discussed our plans for the next day. We would be driving 20 minutes north to Magdala.

MAGDALA

Of late, I seem to be having an unexpected friendship with one of the "bad girls" of the Bible, Mary Magdalene. In the introduction to

This St. Peter fish—better known as tilapia outside of Israel—was caught in the Sea of Galilee mere hours before it was cooked. If you are a seafood lover, it is easy to get your fill in Israel, but get used to your food looking back at you. Fish cooked on the bone tends to be more flavorful than fillets.

my last book, I tell the story of how I discovered in a rather embarrassing way during graduate school that Mary Magdalene was *not* a prostitute, as I had been told my entire life. The tradition began on September 14, 1591, when Pope Gregory conflated Mary of Bethany, Mary of Magdala, and the woman who washes Jesus's feet in Luke 7:37-50. Gregory told all the Christians that the seven demons taken out of Mary Magdalene represented the seven vices, and that perfume used to wash Jesus's feet was formerly used "to perfume her flesh in forbidden acts."[1] With the pope as God's representative on earth, no one questioned Gregory's statements or seemed to notice that Scripture did not agree with what he said. Her false reputation as a sinful sex worker is an example of how humans' traditions can sometimes get confused or conflated with actual Scripture.

I had spent the first 22 years of my life imagining her as a sinful, poor, pitiable creature, when in fact she was an independent woman from a wealthy city, who was close to the apostles and Jesus. Visiting her hometown of Magdala would reinforce this historical and scriptural truth.

The First-Century City

Standing on the shore of the Sea of Galilee next to a replica of a first-century fishing boat, it is easy to imagine Jesus and His disciples docking at Magdala's port (Matthew 15:39) before taking a short walk to the synagogue to preach as He had throughout Galilee (Matthew 4:23).

In the Bible, Jesus leaves the feeding of the 4,000 and sails to Magdala (Matthew 15:39). Assuming that Matthew is telling his story in chronological order, it is there that the Pharisees and Sadducees ask Him to "show them a sign from heaven" (Matthew 16:1).

Only the Gospel of Luke describes His encounter with Mary:

> [Jesus] went through every city and village, preaching and bringing the glad tidings of the kingdom of God. And the twelve were with Him, and certain women who had been healed of evil spirits and infirmities—Mary called Magdalene, out of whom had come seven demons, and Joanna the wife of Chuza, Herod's steward, and Susanna, and many others who provided for Him from their substance (Luke 8:1-3).

We learn two things from Luke: Mary Magdalene was delivered from the possession of seven demons, and she was among the wealthy women who traveled with and supported Jesus's ministry. Her encounter with Jesus certainly changed her life, as she stayed with Him up to and through His death and resurrection according to all four Gospels. In fact, she is the only person whom Matthew, Mark, Luke, and John all agree found Jesus's tomb to be empty.

Archaeologists have discovered that Magdala first became a city around 200 BCE. By the time Mary was born, it had grown into a prosperous fishing village with a distinctly Jewish culture. It boasts the oldest synagogue discovered in Galilee to date, and the frescoed walls and mosaic floors preserved in several buildings survived flooding, conquest, and a major earthquake. Four high-quality, groundwater-fed ritual baths further indicate the importance of the Jewish religion to daily life, and the large marketplace testifies to the city's great wealth.

The current excavation of Magdala began in 2009, when contractors preparing the foundation of a new building stumbled on the remains of that first-century synagogue. The dig is now jointly sponsored by the Israel Antiquities Authority and two Mexican universities, Universidad Anáhuac México Sur and Universidad Autónoma de Mexico. It was seen by Pope Benedict XVI in 2009 and is visited by more and more Jewish and Christian tourists each year.[2]

Today visitors can enjoy a mostly do-it-yourself tour thanks to helpful diagrams and historic facts presented throughout the site. Once excavation and restoration are complete, Magdala will be a dazzling example of maritime society in the ancient world.

> To enhance your reading experience, visit **www.magdala.org**. There you will find official photographs and stories from the excavation.

The Modern Institute

I was pleasantly surprised to see how dedicated Magdala's scholars are to "rehabilitating" Mary Magdalene's reputation. Alongside Magdala's dig site is the Magdalena Institute, a nonprofit inspired by the figure of Mary Magdalene that seeks "to highlight issues of human dignity—with an emphasis on the dignity of women—and contributions of the feminine genius in both religious history and facets of life today."[3] Many scholars would argue that the denigration of Mary by Pope Gregory (and the subsequent centuries of teachers and preachers who solidified her identification as a prostitute) is the result of historic misogyny in the church. The Institute works from the same place where Mary walked and Jesus may have preached to make sure no woman is marginalized because of her gender.

Alongside the excavation site and the Institute, the New Gate to Peace foundation is busy building a visitors' center, a seaside worship center, and a guesthouse. A chapel is already on-site. The added tourism these ventures will bring to the modern city of Magdala will be appreciated by the local residents as Jewish and Christian religious groups make it a place for retreats and conventions. Today, the once-prosperous city is a blink-and-you'll-miss-it stop between Tiberias and Capernaum. But it is a stop worth making.

CAPERNAUM

Our visit to Capernaum was lovely, but not quite as thorough as we would have liked. This site has split ownership: The Franciscans own the archaeological excavations, while the Israel Nature and Parks Authority maintains the park. Unbeknownst to us, we arrived the afternoon before a holiday, so we could only access the very windy park.

During the first century, Capernaum was a bustling fishing village, part of a heavily trafficked trading route, and home to a Roman garrison. It is frequently the setting of Jesus's activities as described in the Gospels. He did the following there:

- lived during much of His ministry (Matthew 14:13; Mark 2:1)
- performed many miracles (Matthew 8:5-13; Mark 1:21-28; 2:1-12; Luke 7:1-10; John 4:46-54)
- paid taxes (Matthew 17:24)
- taught in the synagogue (Mark 1:21; Luke 4:31-38)
- walked on water (Matthew 14:22-34; Mark 6:45-53; John 6:16-20)
- selected Simon Peter, Andrew, John, James Zebedee, and Matthew as apostles (Matthew 4:18-22; 9:9-13; Mark 2:13-17; Luke 5:1-11,27-28)

Archaeologists have found the remains of a residential quarter that stood between 100 BCE and 746 CE, when a large earthquake hit the area. Many of the homes were built out of basalt (as was the restaurant), likely because it was an easily accessible local stone. The area was "mixed use," as our local governments would zone it today, meaning retail and residential coexisted.

In the 400s CE, the local Christians built a shrine around a first-century structure that may have been used as a home church. A century earlier, a Christian pilgrim named Lady Egeria had identified the first-century structure as Peter's house, which had subsequently been renovated and upgraded to a home church. The archaeologists found that the original house had been covered in plaster and graffitied with Christian messages such as "Lord Jesus help your servant" and "Christ have mercy" in various languages. At the same time, the utensils used there changed from domestic pottery such as cookware and bowls to only storage jars and lamps. People gathered there; they no longer cooked or slept there.[4] The fifth-century shrine was destroyed in the seventh century, but the Franciscans built a new church, St. Peter's Church, over the area in the 1990s to preserve the artifacts of what may or may not be Peter's actual home.[5]

> Now when Jesus had come into Peter's house, He saw his wife's mother lying sick with a fever. So He touched her hand, and the fever left her. And she arose and served them (Matthew 8:14-15).

Leaving Capernaum's park, we could see a green-domed monastery on a hill above us. Built by the Catholic Church for Franciscan nuns in the 1930s, just as the Greek Orthodox church was finishing the Church of the Apostles down on the coastline, this airy octagonal building takes advantage of the natural and landscaped scenery around it.[6] Naturally, we arrived at the church just in time for its gates to close. No Trespassing signs were posted everywhere, so we missed our chance to view the Sea of Galilee from the spot Lady Egeria identified as the place where Jesus gave His most famous sermon, the Sermon on the Mount (Matthew 5–7), which included such greatest hits as the Beatitudes, the Lord's Prayer, and the Golden Rule.

ON THE SEA OF GALILEE

Tiberias doesn't get much ink in the New Testament; the city is mentioned only one time as the place from which many of Jesus's listeners set off to look for Him (John 6:23). But it is obvious that the people of Tiberias were frequent trade partners with the more-famous cities to their north: Magdala and Capernaum.

Today Tiberias is a resort town for Israelis and not just a subject for scholarly research or a peaceful stop for pilgrims. My family was reminded of that every evening as multiple party boats would set off and outdoor bars would play music and sports on their giant televisions just below our balconies.

> What is that body of water to the north of the Jordan River? It has had many names. Today, many people call it the Sea of Galilee because it is in the Galilee region of Israel, but it is also known as Lake Tiberias and Lake Kinneret, after two historic cities on its shores. In the Bible, it is sometimes called Lake Gennesaret (a word that is related to *Kinneret* and means something like "garden of riches"[7]). But what *is* it—a sea or a lake? As a large body of fresh water that is basically landlocked, most people agree it is actually a lake. Ancients who may have never seen an ocean or the Mediterranean Sea may have called it a sea because of its vast size and sometimes-turbulent waters.

I found myself equally aggravated at the noise and envious of the sailors. I absolutely love being on (and in) the water, but we did not have the opportunity to sail on the Sea of Galilee. As I was planning our trip, the only tourist excursions on the Sea of Galilee that I could find were designed for church groups of 50-plus people. They sail onto the lake and have worship services for a couple of hours. I had thought I'd be able to find a guide to take just the four of us out once we got to Tiberias, but that didn't happen for two reasons: We ran out of time, and my three travel companions have each suffered seasickness in the past. After forcing my aquaphobic mom to bob in the Dead Sea, I wasn't going to push her onto a boat!

The last evening we were in Tiberias, sitting on my parents' balcony drinking wine we had just bought from vineyards in the Upper Galilee, David observed, "It is really easy to hear what is happening on those boats way out on the lake. I bet that is why Jesus spoke to the multitudes from a boat, instead of just standing in front of them on the shore." He was thinking of two passages in the Gospels, where Jesus makes a seemingly strange decision to get farther away from His audience before He speaks to them:

> Again He began to teach by the sea. And a great multitude was gathered to Him, so that He got into a boat and sat in it on the sea; and the whole multitude was on the land facing the sea (Mark 4:1).

> So it was, as the multitude pressed about Him to hear the word of God, that He stood by the Lake of Gennesaret, and saw two boats standing by the lake; but the fishermen had gone from them and were washing their nets. Then He got into one of the boats, which was Simon's, and asked him to put out a little from the land. And He sat down and taught the multitudes from the boat (Luke 5:1-3).

David had studied some acoustical engineering in college, so he went on to explain to my parents and me that the hills around the sea form a natural amphitheater, much like the Red Rocks Amphitheater we so love outside of Denver, Colorado. Sound also carries more easily over water than it does over land. In 1974, researchers tested the acoustics of the Sea of Galilee in a cove at Capernaum and found that when a balloon was popped over the water at the center of the cove, it could be easily heard 80 meters away (and apparently scared a lot of tourists!).[8] This was great for the multitudes who gathered to hear Jesus, but not so great if a family was hoping for a quiet evening watching the sun set.

Naturally, our conversation turned to the story of Jesus walking on the Sea of Galilee. As we had approached Tiberias a few days earlier, my father had commented that the Sea of Galilee was a lot bigger than he had expected it to be. Of course, the "sea" isn't a sea at all; it is a freshwater lake measuring 13 miles long, 7 miles wide, and 157 feet deep. Because of droughts and siphoning, it has stayed between 6.5 and 13 feet below its natural surface elevation over the last ten years.[9]

In some of my earliest undergraduate theology classes, I remember studying the "walking on water" scene:

> Now in the fourth watch of the night Jesus went to [the disciples who were in the boat], walking on the sea. And when the disciples saw Him walking on the sea, they were troubled, saying, "It is a ghost!" And they cried out for fear.
>
> But immediately Jesus spoke to them, saying, "Be of good cheer! It is I; do not be afraid."
>
> And Peter answered Him and said, "Lord, if it is You, command me to come to You on the water."
>
> So He said, "Come." And when Peter had come down out of the boat, he walked on the water to go to Jesus. But when he saw that the wind was boisterous, he was afraid; and beginning to sink he cried out, saying, "Lord, save me!"
>
> And immediately Jesus stretched out His hand and caught him, and said to him, "O you of little faith, why did you doubt?" And when they got into the boat, the wind ceased.
>
> Then those who were in the boat came and worshiped Him, saying, "Truly You are the Son of God."
>
> When they had crossed over, they came to the land of Gennesaret (Matthew 14:25-34).

There were several theories as to how Jesus could have done so in a nonmiraculous way:

- He was actually standing at the shoreline.
- He was walking on rocks just below the surface.
- The lake was frozen.
- The story is pure allegorical fiction.

Only Matthew tells the story of Peter walking on water; Mark and John only describe the part where Jesus enters the boat and the seas calm. Without Matthew's version, it might be tempting to believe Jesus walking on water wasn't a miracle. As some miracle-averse scholars suggest, stormy skies could have obscured the disciples' views and depth perceptions so they thought He was on the surface of the water and not walking on something firm just beneath it. But there really is no natural explanation they can give for Peter's experience. He could not be walking along the shore and suddenly start to sink in an inch of water. He could not have been sailing on liquid water one minute, stepping out onto ice the next, and then sailing on water back to shore. Lakes can't freeze and unfreeze that quickly, especially when the waters have been so recently tossed by a storm.

Miracles are impossible for some people to accept because they require us to be comfortable with not knowing everything. How did Jesus and Peter walk on water? Since science can't explain it, we must choose to either reject Scripture as fiction or suspend our disbelief and have faith. Ironically, that is the moral of Peter's story. We must have faith in God even when it doesn't make sense and we don't understand how He works.

CHAPTER 6

WINE, WAR, AND WALLS IN THE GOLAN HEIGHTS

ISRAEL'S WINE REGIONS

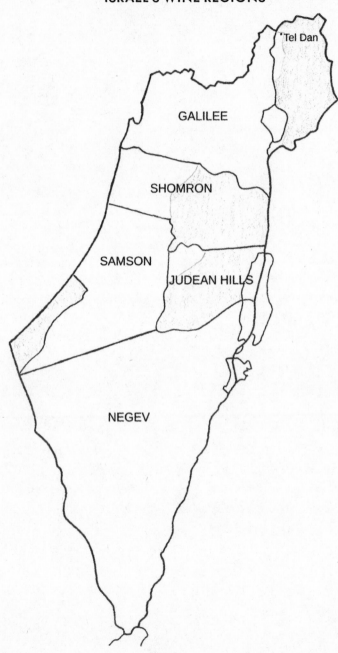

*Tel Dan

GALILEE

SHOMRON

SAMSON

JUDEAN HILLS

NEGEV

According to Scripture, the first thing Noah did after exiting the ark was plant a vineyard (Genesis 9:20). Neither his ark nor his vineyard have ever been identified, but the oldest wine in the world was found in Tbilisi, Georgia, in a 6000 BCE Neolithic village.[1] Only 60 miles from eastern Turkey's Mount Ararat, where the Bible says the ark landed, evidence of the oldest wine industry from 4000 BCE has been found in southeast Armenia, complete with fermentation jars, a winepress, and remains of cultivated grapes.[2]

Winemakers will tell you that the best regions for growing wine grapes fall between the 30N and 48N latitude lines. Israel lies in the lower half of that range, giving it five distinct growing regions: Galilee (home to the Golan Heights, Upper Galilee, and Lower Galilee), the Judean Hills, Samson (the coastal plains and Judean lowlands), Shomron (the region around Mount Carmel), and Negev. Each region is distinguished by its particular soil compositions, rainfall amounts, and altitude.[3]

Based on ancient artwork, letters, utensils, and organic remains, we can tell that wine was an important trading commodity in Israel from at least 3500 BCE. The Bible itself frequently mentions wine throughout both testaments. In 1 Kings 21, a vintner from the Jezreel Valley (just southwest of Nazareth) had his land stolen by the Northern King-dom's monarchs, Ahab and Jezebel:

> Naboth the Jezreelite had a vineyard which was in Jezreel, next to the palace of Ahab king of Samaria. So Ahab spoke to Naboth, saying, "Give me your vineyard, that I may have it for a vegetable garden, because it is near, next to my house; and for it I will give you a vineyard better than it. Or, if it seems good to you, I will give you its worth in money."
>
> But Naboth said to Ahab, "The LORD forbid that I should give the inheritance of my fathers to you!"
>
> So Ahab went into his house sullen and displeased because of the word which Naboth the Jezreelite had spoken to him...
>
> Then Jezebel his wife said to him, "You now exercise author-ity over Israel! Arise, eat food, and let your heart be cheer-ful; I will give you the vineyard of Naboth the Jezreelite." And she wrote letters in Ahab's name, sealed them with his seal, and sent the letters to the elders and the nobles who were dwelling in the city with Naboth. She wrote in the letters, saying,
>
>> Proclaim a fast, and seat Naboth with high honor among the people; and seat two men, scoundrels, before him to bear witness against him, saying, "You have blasphemed God and the king." Then take him out, and stone him, that he may die.
>
> ...And it came to pass, when Jezebel heard that Naboth had been stoned and was dead, that Jezebel said to Ahab, "Arise, take possession of the vineyard of Naboth the Jezree-lite, which he refused to give you for money; for Naboth is not alive, but dead." So it was, when Ahab heard that Naboth was dead, that Ahab got up and went down to take possession of the vineyard of Naboth the Jezreelite (1 Kings 21:1-11,14-16).

Aside from highlighting the sociopathic behavior of the Northern Kingdom's most notorious queen, this story indicates just how important vineyards were to the ancient state. Presumably, Ahab wanted this particular patch of land for two reasons: It was near the city's administrative center, and its vines were old.[4] Old vines make better wine. And more wine. Ahab would have wanted that good wine for his own lavish parties at the palace and (probably more importantly) as a commodity to trade with the neighboring Assyrians.

The wine industry flourished in the region until the rule of the Ottomans, which lasted from 1516 to 1917. The Muslim empire prohibited the production of wine within their borders, and indigenous wine-grape varieties literally died out. In the mid-nineteenth century, as Zionism was surging in Europe and Asia and Jews were moving back to Palestine, grapevines from France and Italy were transplanted to the various growing regions.[5] It has taken time for the "new" vines to establish themselves, but today Israel boasts some of the best wine in the world.

During our tours, the vineyards were all beginning their annual grape harvests.

Several months before we left for Israel, I contacted Israel Wine Experience, a wine tour company led by Oded Shoham.[6] We would learn that Oded was born in Israel, raised outside of Chicago, and then returned to Israel as an adult. He is himself a vintner, and he led our tour personally. We had agreed that he would take us on a daylong tour, including two wineries in the Golan region. I had also asked that we visit Tel Dan, a nature reserve on the Lebanese border with important archaeological significance. He obliged.

After he picked us up in a comfortable SUV, we drove for 45 minutes around the southern tip of the Sea of Galilee and up to Chateau Golan. The conversation was mostly getting-to-know-you stuff, but we did talk a bit about the wine industry as a whole in Israel. It functions as most other countries' wine productions do—grow the grapes, harvest the grapes, ferment and bottle the juice, sell the wine—but with two peculiarities. First, special attention must be taken to create kosher wine, which is understandably in demand in Israel. Second, international sales are not simple.

Oded explained to us that when we got to the first winery, it would be very important that we not touch anything because Chateau Golan produces kosher wine. When I hear the word *kosher*, I think about what observant Jews are not allowed to eat—specifically pork, shellfish, and meat with dairy. So from the third row of the SUV, I piped up, "Isn't wine already kosher?" Oded explained that observant Jews require that kosher wine never come into contact with anything or anyone considered unclean. From the planting to the bottling, only Sabbath-keeping Jews are allowed to touch the product or the tools that produce it. Not even Oded could touch anything inside because he considers himself a secular Jew.

The requirement that only certain people come in contact with kosher products (wine or otherwise) is an ancient law that comes from the Hebrew Bible. Pagan people surrounding the Hebrews, such as the Egyptians and Canaanites, used wine in the rituals for their gods. According to the Jewish rabbis who standardized kosher laws, God did not want wine that had been used in pagan rituals to be reused as libations to Him or drunk by His people. Those early rabbis later extended this ban to any wine that had been handled by a non-Jew.[7]

At the heart of the Bible's purity laws is the idea that nothing unholy, not one speck of anything unholy, can coexist with holiness. A smidge of "unclean" dirties anything clean. An excellent example of this principle is on display in 2 Samuel 6:6-7:

> When they came to Nachon's threshing floor, Uzzah put out his hand to the ark of God and took hold of it, for the oxen stumbled. Then the anger of the LORD was aroused against Uzzah, and God struck him there for his error; and he died there by the ark of God.

That verse has bothered me for most of my life because I understood that passage as describing the death of a well-meaning Israelite who was trying to save the ark from falling. Surely I would have wanted to do the same in Uzzah's position. But what actually happened there was a collision of purity and impurity. Unclean humans cannot come into physical contact with a perfect God (or in that case, His holy seat) and survive.

Don't expect to see "Golan Heights" on any wine labels at your local liquor store. Exporters use the designation "Upper Galilee" if they want their wines to sell outside of Israel.

Oded told us that the international community has begun boycotting Israeli wine, especially wines from the Golan Heights and West Bank,[8] because of Israel's financial and legal support of Israelis settling within the regions controlled by the Palestinian Authority. Winemakers in Golan, regardless of their religious affiliations, fear that soon they will no longer be able to sell their bottled wines outside of Israel at all.

ON THE DISPUTED BORDERS

The history of Israel's modern borders is as changeable and confusing as the history of its ancient borders. In the Bible, Israel is at its

largest under King Solomon when all 12 tribes are described as a uni-
fied country, he has made many foreign alliances through marriages,
and his cities are well fortified. Under his reign only, Israel was over
twice the size that it is today.

After Solomon's death around 930 BCE, Israel had a civil war that
resulted in the formation of the Northern Kingdom (also called Israel
or Samaria) and the Southern Kingdom (also called Judah). Skirmishes
between the two kingdoms kept their internal boundary in flux until
outside empires such as Assyria, Babylon, Persia, and Rome would
wholly conquer the land again and again over the next millennium.
After 300 years as part of the Byzantine Empire, Israel would be held
by the Muslim Arabs (636–1099 CE), the Christian Crusaders (1099–
1291), the Mamluks (1291–1516), the Ottoman Empire (1516–1917),
and finally, the British (1917–1948).

Still with me? The map is about to get even more confusing.

The modern State of Israel was founded on May 14, 1948, when
David Ben Gurion declared the existence of the new Jewish state. The
next day, new Israel was attacked from all sides: Egypt, Jordan, Syria,
and Lebanon, who were all helped by Iraq. After almost a year of fighting, Israel had gained 40 percent more ground from its neighbors than
it had before the war, much of which they ceded to their neighbors at
the armistice. Egypt controlled the Gaza Strip, Jordan controlled the
West Bank, and the borders between those areas and Israel were called
the Green Line. (We will talk more about those two areas' current status in chapter 8.)

In 1967, Israel was again attacked by its Arab neighbors in what has
been called the Six-Day War. Israel took Gaza and the entire Sinai Peninsula from Egypt, the West Bank from Jordan, and the Golan Heights
from Syria. In peace accords, it would return most of that land to the
aggressor nations.

Israel kept the region of the Golan Heights, which Syria tried to
take back by force in 1973. In spite of the armistice agreement that
left most of the area in Israel's control, both nations still claim the area.
Israel officially annexed it in 1981, but the international community
does not recognize that annexation.[9] Since then, there has been little

Between October 6 and 25, 1973, in what many call the Yom Kippur War, Egypt and Syria simultaneously attacked Israel on their northern and southern borders. Israel won land in both directions, almost coming within sight of Cairo and Damascus.

conflict regarding the Golan Heights, mainly because its citizens are Arab and not Palestinian. Israel has offered citizenship to everyone who lives there, but few have taken it. And the Syrian civil war has distracted the Syrian regime and consumed their resources. Any desire in Syria to recover the Golan is way on the back burner.[10]

Prior to the start of the civil war in 2011, archaeologists were active in more than 100 digs inside Syria.[11] Its land is part of the Fertile Crescent, also called the Cradle of Civilization, where scientists believe the earliest humans began agrarian lifestyles.

For the Bible reader, Syria can be roughly equated to the Old Testament land of the Arameans. It lay to the north of the Northern Kingdom and frequently warred with its southern neighbor. About ten years before they would conquer the Northern Kingdom of Israel, the Assyrian empire conquered Aram and its capital of Damascus, deported its high-ranking citizens, and resettled it with people from other nations they had already conquered (2 Kings 16:9). Northern Israel would suffer the same fate in 722 BCE (2 Kings 17:5). In the New Testament,

Damascus is most famous as the place where Saul was converted and began his Christian ministry (Acts 9:1-25).

As the civil war rages on, many archaeological treasures are being lost, sometimes by accident and sometimes on purpose. The American Society of Oriental Research (ASOR) has a department dedicated to monitoring endangered antiquities. Since 2014, they have reported the damage of multiple sites and the illegal excavations of others.[12] It seems antiquities can be valuable in different ways. Unearthed artifacts can be sold for funds, and excavated sites make great shelters if one assumes the enemy will not want to destroy historical sites.

An ancient temple, roughly contemporary with Solomon's temple in Jerusalem, was destroyed by Turkish forces on January 22, 2018. The temple at Ain Dara held particular interest for biblical archaeologists because of its parallels with the descriptions of the first temple in the Bible; it gave us a kind of glimpse into what Solomon had created, complete with three chambers, statues of cherubim, and carvings of fruit. Two craters are now in the temple, and the iconic giant footprints at its threshold have been destroyed. Remains indicate precision weapons were used in the strike, but the international community has not determined if the strike was intended to destroy the temple because of its cultural significance or because enemy combatants were hiding within it.[13]

Live ammunition and abandoned bunkers remain in the DMZ between Israel and Syria.

Today it is hard to imagine that we will ever be able to cross the rows of electrified, barbed-wire fences that mark the borders between Syria and Israel. It seems the area has been the setting of all too many wars since civilization was born there, and modern conflicts are rapidly erasing the archaeological evidence of the ancients' lives.

INSIDE TEL DAN

Near the point where Lebanon, Syria, and Israel meet is an oasis that has been inhabited for the last 7,000 years and is both the literal and figurative northern border of Israel: the city of Dan. Judges 18 describes how Dan (one of the 12 tribes of Israel that had been allotted land near the Philistines but had been unable to take it for themselves) moved to Laish, conquered the Canaanite city, and began the on-again, off-again pagan worship that would plague Israel throughout the Hebrew Bible (Judges 18:1-2,27-29).

The city of Dan was established well before David's and Solomon's United Monarchy, and worship of God was technically legal there until the first temple was finished (see chapter 2). But as soon as Solomon died and a civil war split Israel into the Northern and Southern Kingdoms around 930 BCE, King Jeroboam built ritual centers at Dan and another city, Bethel, fearing his people's annual pilgrimages to Jerusalem might make them want to reunite with the Southern Kingdom. And in each of those temples he placed a golden calf where the ark should have been.

> Jeroboam said in his heart, "Now the kingdom may return to the house of David: If these people go up to offer sacrifices in the house of the LORD at Jerusalem, then the heart of this people will turn back to their lord, Rehoboam king of Judah, and they will kill me and go back to Rehoboam king of Judah."
>
> Therefore the king asked advice, made two calves of gold, and said to the people, "It is too much for you to go up to Jerusalem. Here are your gods, O Israel, which brought you

up from the land of Egypt!" And he set up one in Bethel, and the other he put in Dan. Now this thing became a sin, for the people went to worship before the one as far as Dan. He made shrines on the high places, and made priests from every class of people, who were not of the sons of Levi (1 Kings 12:26-31).

Archaeologists have found a temple complex, sacrificial altars, and offering bowls at Dan's cultic site that support the Bible's identification of it as a high place. The earliest pieces date to around the time of Jeroboam, and excavations have shown the site was used for worship practices until the Roman period.[14]

Dan's rich cultic history is fascinating, but this bastion of illegal Northern Israelite worship is now more famous for its confirmation of the United Monarchy. In 1993, archaeologists found broken fragments of a *stele* (that is, a stone tablet with an inscription) that provide the first mention of King David outside of the Bible. In this ancient version of a Facebook post, an Aramean king brags that he destroyed several thousand Israelite and Judahite cavalrymen with the help of his god, Hadad. He then killed their kings. The pieces of the stele do not name any of the men involved in this war, but most scholars associate the document with Hazael of Damascus, who defeated both Jehoram of Israel and Ahaziah of Judah (2 Kings 8–9).[15]

The most interesting part of the find is one phrase: "king of the house of David." When Aram defeated the Southern Kingdom, he didn't call it Judah or Jerusalem or Southern Israel; he called it the "house of David." One hundred years after he died, the divided kingdoms' enemies still recognized David as the founder of Israel. Thirty years after this stele was created, the Northern Israelite King Ahab reconquered Dan, destroyed the brag sheet, and used it to build a wall.[16]

I first learned about this discovery while I was an undergraduate student at Rhodes College. My religious studies professors were skeptical of the Tel Dan stele for two reasons: The writing is not perfectly clear, and the stele was not discovered *in situ*. They and many other scholars at the time believed that David did not exist and Israel never had a

The judge's seat within the Israelite gate at Tel Dan.

United Monarchy, largely because no extrabiblical evidence of David had ever been found. Or, if David and Solomon were historical figures, these scholars would argue, they were more like judges than kings.

This theory is called the *low chronology*, and we will investigate it more in the next chapter. It claims that the great building projects and political power the Bible attributes to David and Solomon were actually achieved by the later independent kings of the North and South, and that the two great kings are in the Bible not as historical figures but as aspirational characters. But in Galilee, we are about to see one of Solomon's greatest achievements—Megiddo—a complete and powerful city whose existence challenges that waning theory, and will one day witness the last battle on earth.

CHAPTER 7

ROLLING THROUGH GALILEE

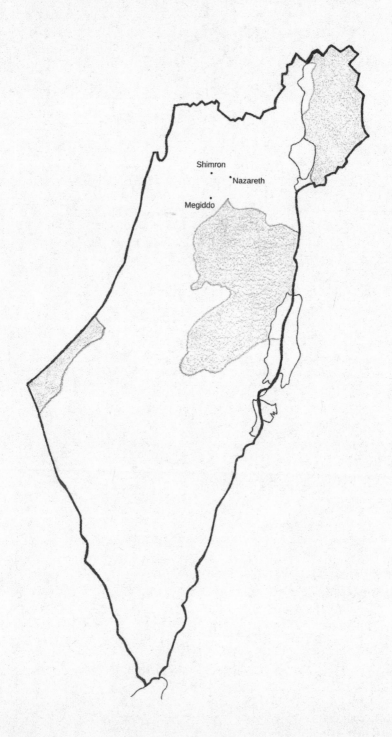

I knew it was going to be a tiring day. We had about ten hours to visit three cities and make it from Tiberias to Jerusalem traveling the long-way-round the West Bank region. So we "got rolling" early that morning.

The name *Galilee* comes from the Hebrew root verb *gll*, meaning "to roll," which is appropriate in several ways. Certainly, the name "rolls" off the tongue, and Galilee's landscape "rolls" more than the rest of Israel's. But the "rolling" from which the word *Galilee* derives seems to have a more political administrative bend. The verb is used to describe scrolls closing, doors swinging, and regions being outlined. It is all about circles, circuits, and cylinder seals.

Galilee has been "redistricted" almost countless times in its history. As a mountainous region with many fertile valleys, it is ideal for both agriculture and warfare. Armies could gain tactical advantages in the heights while communities lived and thrived mostly in the lower elevations. Empire after empire conquered the land for thousands of years, a fact attested to by literary records, biblical and otherwise, as well as artifacts discovered in tels all around the region.

CYLINDER SEALS

The word *seal* first appears in the Song of Moses (Deuteronomy 32), a poem that describes the Hebrews' time wandering in the wilderness. After likening a foreign army's wickedness to spoiled wine from Sodom, God asks, "Is this [spoiled wine] not laid up in store with Me, sealed up among My treasures?" (verse 34). In other places in the Bible, a seal represents the signature of a noble (e.g., 1 Kings 21:8; Nehemiah 10:1) or legalizes an important document (e.g., Jeremiah 32:10-11; Revelation 5–7).

In the ancient world, there were two types of seals: stamp seals (like the signet rings you see being pressed into melted wax in historical dramas) and cylinder seals (which are more like textured paint rollers). An official would put a blob of mud on an opening, be it the edge of a scroll or the hinge of a door, and either press in the stamp or roll the cylinder across. Once dry, the seal was indelible until it was purposefully cracked open. The seals were so strong that they are found intact all over ancient Near Eastern archaeological sites long after the scrolls they held closed have biodegraded.

While stamps usually produced seals that were round or oval—more like the embossed stickers on the backs of Hallmark envelopes or the debossed wax seals of medieval kings—the cylinder seal made a rectangle. The next time you do some home improvement, take your wet paint roller and roll it along the wall for one revolution. That is how cylinder seals were made. But they were far more decorative than your flat, satin, or glossy mark. Each cylinder would be intricately and uniquely carved for its owner, with images representing his name or maybe honoring his deity. When rolled across wet mud, the image would appear in an almost three-dimensional relief, denoting ownership, authority, and security.

TEL SHIMRON

Not every city in Galilee has enjoyed biblical fame. The city of Shimron (that's Shim-RONE, like the Rhone River in France, not Shim-RON as I still sometimes mispronounce it) is only mentioned in the book of Joshua, first as part of a huge Canaanite coalition against Israel:

> When King Jabin of Hazor heard what Israel had done to the central and southern cities of Canaan, he sent messengers to King Jobab of Madon, the *king of Shimron*, the king of Achshaph, and the kings who were in the northern hill country…and to all those who could still fight the invaders. They banded together and came out to fight—so many warriors that you could no more count them than you could count the grains of sand on a beach—and leading them was a vast number of horses and chariots. All of these kings pooled their forces, and they camped together by the waters of Merom, ready to make war on Israel (Joshua 11:1-5 THE VOICE, emphasis added).

A few chapters later, it is named as a conquered city belonging to the Israelite tribe of Zebulun after that Canaanite coalition failed to defeat the invading Israelites (Joshua 19:10-15).

But don't think its relative anonymity means it was small or insignificant. As Daniel Master explained when asked why he wanted to lead an excavation there, "Tel Shimron is important because it was almost constantly occupied starting in 3000 BCE, was a large city on a significant trade route that joined the coastal region of Israel to the Jezreel Valley, and has never before been disrupted."[1] Shimron is in fact the largest site in the Jezreel Valley, larger than its more famous sister to the south, Megiddo.[2]

The day that we traveled from the Sea of Galilee to our next hotel-home in Jerusalem, I took my family to the tel so they could see where I'd been doing voluntary hard labor for the last few weeks. I drove up to the locked gate—where a security guard should have been on duty—ready to explain that I had received special permission to walk around the grids that day. Seeing no one but a goatherd with his animals off in the distance, we locked the car and ducked under the gate.

Little evidence of the once-bustling excavation remained. The trailers and storage containers that had formed the pottery compound had been moved off-site for the winter, as had the water spigot I'd been hoping to open for us that hot day. The exposed grids had been prepared for the coming rains and the constant dirt bikers who rode their self-made trails up and down the tel each afternoon. For the protection of the sites as well as any curious humans who might wander in, tall wire fences were locked around each of the grids and exposed ancient architecture had been packed with sandbags. The winter rains would still melt the exposed earth, creating a layer of soil that volunteers would need to scrape off at the start of the next season, but the excavation had done its best to prevent disturbances for the next ten months.

It felt a bit lonely and sad, walking around by ourselves. I wish David and my parents had been able to see Tel Shimron when all of the volunteers were present, sunshades were up, and 1990s pop music was streaming. Instead, we wandered from grid to grid, from the bottom

The grid is deeper than it looks. By the time the season was over, the balks stood taller than I did.

of the tel where I had worked up to the top where others had dug and a cemetery is open for the public to visit.

NAZARETH

Today, Nazareth is the largest Arab city in Israel. It contains both Muslim and Christian holy sites, but it is not a pilgrimage city for Jews. It is never mentioned in the Hebrew Bible, and most of the times when it appears in the New Testament, it is only as a part of Jesus's epithet, "Jesus of Nazareth," because it was His hometown.

Luke is the only Gospel writer who describes activities occurring in Nazareth. First, Gabriel appears to Mary in Nazareth to tell her she will carry the Christ (Luke 1:26-38). There, "the Child grew and became strong in spirit, filled with wisdom; and the grace of God was upon Him" (Luke 2:40). Later, His neighbors would reject His synagogue teaching and try to throw Him off a cliff, fulfilling His own words to them: "Assuredly, I say to you, no prophet is accepted in his own country" (Luke 4:16-30). Maybe it is a result of how badly He was treated in His hometown that He never returned there, nor did any of His disciples, according to Scripture.

Nazareth's lack of visibility in the Bible and total absence from the Old Testament may be part of the reason why few archaeological digs have been completed there. The State of Israel controls what gets dug, and there are far more important Jewish sites throughout the country. It also doesn't help that every site in Nazareth's Old City that may have any connection to Jesus is covered by a church, so excavations must be completed beneath their foundations. But Israeli archaeologists are used to digging beneath later structures. As we will see at the Temple Mount and the City of David, as much work goes into protecting the existing structures as into the excavations themselves.

The Basilica (or "church") of the Annunciation was built by the Catholic Church in 1969 over the foundations of the ancient village of Nazareth. On the first floor of the church, the traditional home of Mary—a cave—is cared for by Franciscan monks and is the center of daily worship services there. At this spot, tradition says, the archangel

The ancient village of Nazareth was discovered underneath the remains of an eighteenth-century church when it was knocked down to prepare for the current Basilica of the Annunciation.

Gabriel gave his big news to Mary. Towering two stories above the sunken cave is a glorious cupola, decorated with inverted lilies that represent Mary's purity.

Surrounding a courtyard outside this church, which is the largest Catholic church in the Middle East, hang 43 mosaics honoring the annunciation. Each was made by a different country and is done in a unique style that reflects their individual cultures. We were surprised to learn that the United States is not among them.

Just across the street is the Sisters of Nazareth Convent. When the first church was built on the same site by the Byzantine Christians, they believed it to be sheltering the foundations of the house where Jesus grew up. The first-century house had been adorned with mosaics in the fourth-century, and it was identified as His house by a later seventh-century Irish monk, Adomnán of Iona, who had traveled there.[3] There is nothing about the site (or any of Nazareth's other Christian sites) that would prove this is truly the residence of Joseph, Mary, and their children except for scant tradition. But it is nice to think of Jesus growing up so close to his mother's childhood cave-home.

So, there's a church marking the annunciation, a church over Mary's parents' "house," and a church where Jesus grew up. But there is no church marking where Jesus was born in Nazareth. That's because He wasn't born in Nazareth, right? Matthew and Luke both tell us it happened in Bethlehem, while Joseph and Mary were there registering in the Roman Empire's census. I and most Christians have no need to doubt our sacred sources, but some historians aren't so sure.

The Gospels of Mark and John don't have a "birth narrative" for Jesus, so they never state where He was born. When their accounts are read in isolation from the other Gospels, the reader would likely assume that Jesus "of Nazareth" was indeed born in Nazareth. Mark and John give no reason to think differently, and no sources—biblical or otherwise—ever mention Jesus's exact place of birth. (The Church of the Nativity in Bethlehem honors a cave that has been rumored to be His birthplace since the second century, but that is impossible to prove.)

Historians would say that because Mark's is the oldest and least polished of the Gospels, details he mentions about Jesus's origins have a better chance of being accurate; Mark's Gospel had less editing, fewer literary influences, and less time for the author's memory to fade. They would then turn to Matthew and Luke—who name Jesus's birthplace as Bethlehem—and say those writers had an ulterior motive in "moving" Jesus's birth to Bethlehem: so He would fulfill the prophecy. John's Gospel might support this idea, based on his record of some of His early followers debating this very prophecy:

> Therefore many from the crowd, when they heard this saying, said, "Truly this is the Prophet." Others said, "This is the Christ."

> But some said, "Will the Christ come out of Galilee? Has not the Scripture said that the Christ comes from the seed of David and from the town of Bethlehem, where David was?" So there was a division among the people because of Him (John 7:40-43).

The followers' disagreement goes unresolved in John's retelling. No one in the crowd says, "Wait a minute! He *was* born in Bethlehem! He just grew up in Nazareth," as the reader might expect. Maybe no one knew that or thought of it at the time, but some scholars will use the followers' unresolved debate about Jesus's birth in John and Mark's silence as evidence that He was born in Nazareth, Galilee, and not Bethlehem, Judaea.[4]

Looking back at the Basilica of the Annunciation, David and I noticed a giant faded sign that was impossible to miss when looking up at the church's dome. We were a message written in Arabic and English: "And whoever seeks a religion other than Islam, it will never be accepted of him, and in the Hereafter he will be one of the losers.—Holy Quran"

Before my parents saw it, David suggested we do the most stereotypical, annoying-American-tourist thing possible: "There's a McDonald's. Let's go get milkshakes!" It was on our way back to the car, and something cold and familiar sounded good to us all. As we started to cross the street in front of the McDonald's, a group of men standing under a pergola leered at my mother and me. I assumed they were making faces because my head was uncovered and I was walking beside my husband instead of behind him, so I put my head down and pushed David in front of me. At the crosswalk, matters got worse. Young men in their cars started yelling and honking at my mom and me, then they made us think they were going to hit us as we walked by them. This did not fit with the kindness we had experienced a few blocks away when we were stuck in the Arab neighborhood an hour earlier.

I pondered that loud translation of the Quran all the way to the McDonald's, but circumstance soon overtook my deep thoughts. As we walked in the door (to glorious air-conditioning!), we were greeted by six-feet-tall touch-screen menus. Up front we saw employees behind "cash registers," so David and my dad walked up there thinking the employees could just take our order. They sent the guys back to the screens—all transactions at that McDonald's are now fully automated—and we were left to order in either Arabic or Hebrew. Good thing there were lots of pictures! Cold drink in hand, GPS directions loaded, and Nazareth in the rearview mirror, I asked everyone if they had seen that sign posted so boldly underneath the holiest Christian site in Nazareth. I had so many questions. Why was it only in Arabic and English? Was the intention to alienate the Western visitors or to convert them? Was tourism not important to the local economy? Are we safe here?

In Israel, the tension between Muslims and Jews is often palpable. But this was the first time I truly felt unwanted in that country. Sitting in our Mitsubishi Eclipse, we could not answer any of my questions, so I asked everyone one more: "How would you feel about taking a tour of Hebron? It's a little expensive, and it will take an entire day, but we would get to see sites and hear stories that most tourists don't."

My mom was thoughtful; my dad said, "Let's go for it," just as David said, "Nuh-uh." After our next stop at Megiddo, I'd be booking a tour to the West Bank.

MEGIDDO

If you aren't an Old Testament nerd like me, that word, *Megiddo*, may not sound familiar. But I bet its New Testament counterpart will ring a bell: *Armageddon*. They are the names of a place far more famous for its future than its past. There, the final battle will be fought.

The differences in the English spellings between the Old Testament name (mountain of Megiddo) and the New Testament name (Armageddon) result from *transliterations*. Not all languages use the same alphabet. The letters we use in English—which you are reading right now—are from the "Latin alphabet," but other languages have their own unique letters. You know what an *a* looks and sounds like in English, but would you know to speak that sound when you saw an א (Hebrew), α (Greek), or ١ (Arabic)? Those symbols are unspeakable in English, so we need some help.

When an English translator is using a word from a language with a different alphabet without translating its meaning, he or she will substitute the foreign characters with the Latin letters they sound like. This is *transliteration*. It is especially common with proper nouns. For example, English Bible translations print *Isaac* (which sounds like his name when spoken in Hebrew) instead of translating it to "Laughter." My husband's name, David, is also a transliteration from the Hebrew; his name translates to "Beloved," but we call him by the transliterated Hebrew word "David." This is true for most names, no matter the culture.

When John was recording Revelation, he inked a Greek transliteration of the Hebrew proper noun, "mountain of Megiddo," into the Greek characters he spoke. English translators now take his Greek and transliterate it into English: *har-magedon*. Two language changes and three millennia of spelling and pronunciation changes get us from מגידו to "Armageddon."

On our way to the site of ancient Megiddo, which took half an hour too long thanks to some poor signage, we went over the following facts that we knew about the city from the Bible:

- Megiddo was a Canaanite city conquered by Joshua, as was Shimron (Joshua 12:7,20-21).

- Megiddo paid taxes to Solomon (1 Kings 4:7-12).

- Megiddo was among Solomon's greatest architectural achievements (1 Kings 9:15).

- Southern King Ahaziah retreated to and died in Megiddo after being shot by Northern King Jehu (2 Kings 9:27).

- An Egyptian pharaoh killed Southern King Josiah there in 609 BCE (2 Kings 23:29).

- Megiddo is mentioned in a prophecy of Jerusalem's destruction (Zechariah 12:11).

In summary, Megiddo was a strong city during the Bronze and Iron Ages.

In the New Testament, Armageddon is mentioned only once: "And they gathered them together to the place called in Hebrew, Armageddon" (Revelation 16:16). That one little mention has spawned 2,000 years' worth of speculations about the end times. Dissertations have been written and careers have been based on attempts to decode the book of Revelation.

There is no consensus on what the future holds, and I seriously doubt an ancient tablet will be found in the lowest strata of Megiddo (or anywhere else) with battle plans and objective dates. But let's look at what has physically come out of the ground at Megiddo and leave the prophecies to the specialists.

To begin with, it is unsurprising that Megiddo was such a popular place to attack; the location was practically perfect. The 15-acre site sits 60 meters above the surrounding valley and on the trade line that ran between Egypt, Anatolia, and Mesopotamia. From the top of the city, it was easy to see the invaders or caravans who might be approaching. Today, the area surrounding the tel is irrigated farmland, but in antiquity, it would have been the all-too-frequent campsite for invading armies.

Thanks to corroborating evidence from other nations' records, the battle timeline for Megiddo can be rather easily constructed and its importance verified. It is the only city of ancient Israel to appear in all

The foundations of a temple and high place from the Early Bronze (Canaanite) age.

of its neighbors' war annals, and the first battle to appear in recorded history happened there. Egyptian Pharaoh Thutmose III fought a Canaanite coalition there in 1468 BCE, taking the city after a seven-month-long siege. Pharaoh Merneptah tried to take it in 1220 BCE, and then Pharaoh Shoshenq I (whom the Bible calls Shishak) attacked in 924 BCE. The Assyrian king Tiglath-Pileser III captured Megiddo and made it the capital of a district that included Galilee. And in 609 BCE, Egypt's Pharaoh Neco took it back from Assyria and killed Southern King Josiah.[5]

THE WAR TO END ALL WARS?

Megiddo's history ended about the same time the Israelites' did. After the Babylonian and Persian empires took control, Megiddo was basically deserted, waiting to once again be the site of a massive battle that would be the Last Battle.

In 1917, the British general Edmund Allenby fought the Ottoman Turks at Megiddo and won control of the Jezreel Valley. At the end of the first World War, he became known as "Lord Allenby of Megiddo." I can only wonder if he thought his victory would be quickly followed by the Christ's return.

Some of these battles are mentioned in the Bible, and it looks as if it would be easy to fill in the timeline with other biblical battles that don't appear in extrabiblical documents. Megiddo has been well excavated, beginning in 1925 and closing down each time a war broke out in the region. The first excavation was conducted by the University of Chicago's Institute of Oriental Research and funded by none other than John Rockefeller. (As a friend of mine who digs at Megiddo likes to say, "Archaeology is one *expensive* hobby!") Yigael Yadin (of earlier Masada fame) worked there on behalf of Hebrew University between 1960 and 1971; and since 1992, Israel Finkelstein and David Ussishkin have led

Location, location, location! All empires wanted this real estate.

Tel Aviv University's teams. Megiddo has hosted the who's who of professional archaeologists, and the results reflect that. The site has given us immense amounts of information about the ancient world and even changed how some people plot the timeline of Israel.

But no matter how much comes out of the ground, how well it seems to fit with the biblical record, or how beautifully artifacts are preserved and restored, scholars will reach opposing conclusions using the same data. I was surprised when we arrived at the site to see that the park has chosen sides on one of the most controversial arguments: the very existence of kings Saul, David, and Solomon.

THE LOW CHRONOLOGY

Visiting almost every other park and site in Israel, it is impossible to miss the heavy-handed way the Israeli government has chosen to tell the history of Israel's people. Every sign, every pamphlet, and every docent's speech has been worded so that the archaeological facts support the biblical narrative and often the current political one. (We will discuss this more when we visit the City of David.) Knowing this, I expected Megiddo to tell the visitor all about how Solomon was the great builder of military cities, in addition to his glorious work on Jerusalem's temple and fortifications. I was surprised to find their museum doing the exact opposite.

Finkelstein and Ussishkin, the current longtime excavators at Tel Megiddo, are proponents of the *low chronology*.[6] In brief, this new dating system cuts the tenth century out of the timeline and then smushes the eleventh and ninth centuries back together and adjusts the dates down. They argue that, because there is no unimpeachable physical evidence of Saul, David, and Solomon, those kings never existed. The timeline of Israel moved straight from the period of the Judges into the Divided Monarchy, with the caveat that if David did exist, then he was just a judge and not a king. The low chronology says that the wars fought, cities built, and tribes united by those three men according to the Bible, were actually accomplished by the early Northern and Southern kings. The low chronology stipulates that the Bible writers, who wrote everything after 586 BCE while the Jews were in exile and nothing between 1000 and 586 BCE under the Divided Monarchy, constructed the three characters to give their Jewish readers heroes and a shared national memory of a fictional United Monarchy.[7]

Finkelstein and Ussishkin based a lot of their ideas on the carbon dating from and the pottery found at Tel Rehov. Although this site does not appear in the Bible, it is mentioned in several Egyptian records. It was a thriving city with consistent occupation during the time of the United Monarchy, so it was a perfect "test subject" for the new low chronology.[8]

When I was in college, I was taught that the low chronology was the correct chronology; so when I reached Harvard—that known bastion of liberal values—I was surprised to be taught exactly the opposite. Harvard Divinity School, it turned out, was packed with more biblically conservative professors than the Presbyterian school, Rhodes College, had been. My adviser and the director of Ashkelon's excavations, Larry Stager, passionately disagreed with Finkelstein. He saw no justification for ripping an entire century out of history, unless someone was trying to prove his own ideas rather than honestly explain what the archaeology revealed.

The museum you tour before visiting Megiddo's ruins are a testament to the low chronology ideas. Solomon is not credited as its designer and builder, but the Northern King Ahab (and husband to "bad girl" Jezebel) is. But no matter how scholars and park directors interpret the artifacts, it is undeniable that Megiddo was one big and powerful city. It possessed a plastered water reservoir, fortifications and palaces from three distinct nations (Canaan, Israel, and Assyria), temples, tombs, houses, public storage, and most famously, stables for a large cavalry. We were there for almost four hours, following the suggested trails up and down the tel so we could see all that has been excavated.

Visiting this city that was built to endure war after war—be they ancient, twentieth-century, or future—it is obvious that conflict is woven into the fabric of the land. Archaeology and history agree that the area now occupied by the State of Israel has never witnessed peace for long. Yesterday, the Israelites were fighting the Babylonians, Persians, and Romans; today, the Israelis fight Arab nations and the Palestinians. Though the world longs for peace, I cannot imagine a treaty that would actually be able to end the struggle for the land of Abraham, Moses, David, Jesus, and Mohammad. My visit to King David's first capital city, Hebron, in the West Bank would sadly confirm that idea.

CHAPTER 8

FRIEND AND FOE IN HEBRON

Hebron

Near the end of the Tel Shimron dig season, when there was only one weekend left before everyone would go their separate ways, several volunteers in my grid hatched a plan to visit Hebron. (That's heb-RHONE like shim-RHONE, not heb-RON as I've said my entire life.) Over the course of the workweek, the details kept changing. First, they were going to rent a car in Nazareth and drive down, but they learned that they wouldn't be able to take an Israeli rental into the West Bank. Next, they found a local taxi driver who was willing to take them to Hebron for a price that was more than most could afford. Every day there was a new hiccup they addressed with an out-of-the-box solution such as, "We can save money and sleep in the car!"

After six weeks of living in Israel, I think a hard-earned feeling of comfort with our surroundings, previous successful weekends traveling in other Israeli cities, and maybe a dash of that perceived invincibility we all have in our late teens and early twenties kept the participants from acknowledging just how dangerous this outing could be. At second breakfast (that's right, *second breakfast*: Hobbits have nothing on archaeologists who take their breakfasts at 5 a.m. and then again at 9 a.m.!) on the day before the trip was to commence, the leadership of the dig found out about the plans, and the group was strongly encouraged to cancel. At least half of them seemed a bit relieved—what was supposed to be a day's drive in a rented car to visit the Tomb of the Patriarchs had turned into an expensive overnight excursion with a stranger behind the wheel.

In planning my own tour of Israel, I had never really considered going into the West Bank. In my mind, the now frequently visited tourist destinations in Jericho and Bethlehem were still too dangerous because I well remember the bus bombings, kidnappings, and murders that seemed to be on the news every night in the 1990s. And I had never even thought of Hebron as a city I should want to see. My friends were eager to visit the resting places of Abraham, Isaac, and Jacob, but the city's past as Kind David's first capital is just as important.

The evening after my friends' do-it-themselves tour was wisely axed by our dig directors, I got online to book a tour of Hezekiah's Tunnel, which my family and I would go on two weeks later. The City of David website was lined with other tour companies' ads, and I fell down a virtual rabbit hole of tour itineraries. I learned that you can go almost anywhere in Israel and do almost anything in one day as long as you stop and start in Jerusalem. Because of the day's will-they-or-won't-they-go drama, one tour title caught my eye: Hebron Dual Narrative Tour.

> Visit this special city, one of the four holy cities in Judaism and a sacred place in Islam. Our Hebron tour splits the day in two—you'll spend the morning with Jewish "settlers" in the city, and the afternoon in the Palestinian part of the city. By hearing from both sides, this tour will give you a balanced insight on life in Hebron, the city of Abraham, and the site of the burial place of the Biblical Patriarchs and Matriarchs.[1]

The description went on to explain that travel was by "bullet-proof public bus," we would be led by an Israeli guide and a Palestinian guide, and we would have a homemade lunch with a local Palestinian family. *That sounds amazing*, I thought. But I went on to schedule our tour of the City of David and just tucked the idea of taking a guided Hebron tour in the back of my mind. I doubted it would appeal to the rest of my family, and I still wasn't too sure we would be completely safe. Only after my mother's and my experiences in Nazareth did I mention this tour to my family, and everyone cautiously agreed we should go. Visiting the sites of David and the patriarchs would be thrilling, but witnessing life in modern Palestine would be invaluable. I booked our tour for the following day.

ON THE GROUND IN HEBRON

The morning of the tour, the four of us had our earliest wake-up yet. We were scheduled to meet the group at 8:00 a.m. at the Abraham Hostel in Jerusalem, which was about 20 minutes away from our hotel by taxi in the rush-hour traffic. My parents are the people who taught me that "on time" really means "late," so naturally we gave ourselves an entire hour for that part of the trip.

Abraham Tours starts most of its tours from the hostel, so when we arrived with 40 minutes to kill, we found the lobby packed with people of all ages, nationalities, and attire. The group going to Eilat stood out next to us; they were in glorified beachwear, while we were covered from head to toe and carrying extra shawls and scarves. Every few minutes another guide would pipe up and call roll for the group he was about to take. Those people would leave, and their places on the eclectic, comfy couches were quickly taken.

Right on time, Eliyahu McLean started calling roll for the Hebron tour. He was obviously an observant Jew—he had visible *peiyot* curling out of his straw hat and *tzitzit* dangling against his black cargo pants—but his casual street clothes and KEEN hiking sandals didn't quite seem to fit. We would learn that Eliyahu was from, as he called it, "a small country called the people's republic of Berkeley. It has its own foreign policy." He had moved to Israel over 20 years ago and was married to an Israeli woman with five children who liked to tease him about "Daddy's funny American accent." For 22 years, Eliyahu has engaged in interfaith dialogue work; he created this tour of Hebron eight years ago, as soon as he could find a Palestinian who was willing and able to do the H1 side of the tour. That day we would be meeting Moham-mad at the border crossing.

KEEP YOUR SHIRT ON

Before we left the hostel, the tour guide appraised our outfits and sent two women back to change when he saw their shoul-ders and legs were uncovered. One woman was so offended that she didn't go; the other grabbed a long-sleeved button-down that she refused to keep on, and her lack of clothes did create problems for us on the streets of H1.

As I was growing up, anytime I went someplace nice I was told to wear "church clothes." Back in the 1980s and '90s that meant a simple dress, pantyhose (ugh), and Mary Janes, or something like that. But most of us don't dress up for church anymore. Had I told my niece to wear her church clothes the first time I took her to the theater, she would have arrived in everyday streetwear because we all wear jeans and leggings on Sunday mornings. David asks me every Sunday if he can wear a T-shirt—most of the other men do—but I still make him put on a polo. (I'm old-fashioned that way!)

No shorts, nothing sleeveless, and ladies need a head cover-ing. Yes, it is hot as blazes outside, and yes, you'll be a puddle in under five minutes. But your sweat will be recognized as a sign of respect.

Hebron is only 18 miles south of Jerusalem, but it took us over an hour to get there. All of the other tours were jumping on large charter buses (except for two couples going on a Jeep tour of the Negev—how had I missed that?), but we walked to the rail station. He bought our tickets to the bus station, where we climbed into a city bus along with the rest of the general public. He had us all fill the back, and he started the tour immediately, yelling over the traffic noise and airbrakes.

The bus ride from Jerusalem to Hebron is a special route. After leaving Jerusalem, you soon enter two long tunnels. Israel had blasted the bypass under a mountain to protect Israelis who needed to go through Bethlehem and its many refugee camps on the way to Hebron. The parts of the trip that weren't underground were elevated, and razor wire often lined the road just on the edge of the slope. These security measures were put in place because of the violence during the First and Second Intifadas. Jewish passengers on their way to worship at Hebron, the second-holiest city in Judaism, had often been targeted.

While we were still on the road, Eliyahu told us stories of violent kidnappings and murders of Israeli Jews, pointing out the memorials where they had occurred as we sped by. He went on to say, "I jokingly like to call the tour the 'Competing Victimology Tour.' Each of us will try to compete for your sympathies, to prove who's the greater victim. In essence, that is what we both do very well. To the world…I'm gonna put on the victim hat, but I ultimately believe we need to get beyond victim mentality to solve this thing."

Israel's 20 percent (H2)

We got off the cool, air-conditioned bus and stood on the sidewalk. "This is going to be a long day," Eliyahu warned us. We'd be walking several miles up and down the city, and almost all of it would be outside. There is no such thing as ADA compliancy in Hebron, so there were no ramps or elevators. Only thousand-year-old steps, narrow sidewalks, and dirt paths.

We began by walking around the H2 neighborhoods and looking at the many murals Israelis had painted on mostly abandoned buildings. Everything was a memorial to a brutal kidnapping or murder—a reminder of how the world's empires had continually conquered, controlled, and killed the Jews since before they were even called "Jews."

He took us to Beit Hadassah, the first medical center to be built in Israel. Between 1893 and 1929, the Hadassah Jewish women's organization provided free health care to Jews and Arabs there. The building was reclaimed by the H2 community in 1979, and there is now a museum in the basement dedicated to the 1929 massacre. On the first floor is a synagogue, where we sat in a stuffy library while Eliyahu told us the 4,000-year history of Israel—in just over 30 minutes!

Hebron in the Ancient Texts

"People of the Book" is a phrase that originated in the holiest Islamic scriptures, the Qur'an.[2] The Qur'an uses the phrase to refer to Jews and Christians, with whom Muslims share common religious heroes such as Abraham and Moses. Today the phrase is used more broadly in the public square to refer to all three religions, and all three have an important historic connection with Hebron.

The ancient city of Hebron features prominently in the Hebrew Bible. Most famously, it is the home and burial place of Abraham, Isaac, Jacob, and their families (Genesis 13:18; 23:2,19; 35:27; 37:14). The Canaanites who lived there during the Israelites' conquest of the area were "descendants of Anak" whose "giant" size intimidated Caleb's army (Numbers 13:21-33), leaving the city for Joshua to capture later (Joshua 10:36-37; Judges 1:10). David made Hebron his first capital city; he ruled from there for seven and a half years and had six children (2 Samuel 2:11; 3:2-5; 5:1-5). Hebron is also where his son Absalom set up his own government in an attempt to overthrow David (2 Samuel 15:7-12).

Stories of Hebron don't appear in the text of the Qur'an, but Islam has a strong tradition that largely agrees with the biblical narratives about the city. Muslims, too, count Abraham as the patriarch of their religion; they believe that he and his descendants were buried there. This tradition was known to Muhammad, who visited the cave in Hebron during his famous Night Journey from Mecca to Jerusalem. Hebron is the fourth holiest city in Islam because Muhammad stopped there to pay his respects to the father of his religion. He then encouraged his own followers to make pilgrimages there as well.[3]

THE SUPPLEMENTAL SACRED BOOKS IN JUDAISM AND ISLAM

Ask a Christian what Scripture is, and that person will pull out a Bible. All of the holy books are bound together in one place. All divine authority is between those covers. We may supplement our studies with the theological writings of great Christian thinkers, but no one should be holding up the words of Lewis, Calvin, Luther, or even the saints as equal to the Word of God.

In the Jewish tradition, the Hebrew Bible (what Christians call the Old Testament, just in a different order with slightly different verse numbers) is also the only Scripture. But for thousands of years, rabbis have engaged in theological exercises with the Bible and each other. Their words were collected into the *Talmud* and *Midrash*, and a lot of the Jewish traditions and beliefs draw on the writings of those early rabbis. Those sources may not be divine, but they have great authority in Jewish beliefs, traditions, and practices.

Muslims have an even greater number of authoritative texts. For them the Qur'an is the biggie—it contains the exact, unedited words of God as given to and through Muhammad—but they accept other collections of writings as sacred as well. The Hadith contains the words of Muhammad himself and stories of his life as recorded by Muslim clerics from oral tradition; the Sunnah lays out the social and legal practices expected among Muslims. Most of the disagreements between Muslim sects result from the diverging opinions regarding the two secondary sources, as there is no consensus as to which parts are more important than others.

Hebron in the Modern Era

Until 1929, Hebron was a peaceful city where Jews and Arabs had coexisted during the Ottoman era. Under the rule of an empire, all citizens were equally happy or miserable depending on their governor. At that time, neighborhoods were mixed, and everyone shopped in the same stores on the same streets. Jews and Muslims owned businesses together. They were all Hebronites first. And Hebron was the "Philadelphia" of Israel. You see, Hebron and al-Khalil (the city's Arabic name) both mean "beloved friend."

The Hebron Massacre

After World War I, when Great Britain and France took control of the region, all the maps were redrawn. Syria, Lebanon, Jordan, Iraq—all of the Middle East countries' borders were drawn almost willy-nilly. In British Mandatory Palestine, Haj Amin al Husseini was appointed the Grand Mufti of Jerusalem; as the local political official with the highest status, it was his responsibility to interpret Islamic law for everyone who lived in his region.

On Friday, August 23, 1929, during one of his regular radio addresses, he told everyone that the Jews were trying to take over Al-Aqsa Mosque with the help of the British "crusaders." At his instruction, Muslims sprinted en masse for Jerusalem to keep that from happening, but the British turned them back. In reality, the

The Torah scrolls in Avraham Avinu Synagogue were spirited away to Jerusalem in the aftermath of the 1929 massacre. The scrolls were returned in 1985.

Jews were trying to add places to pray at the Western Wall—something that had been discussed for years—but the British played into the grand mufti's narrative by stopping the Muslim crowds from entering Jerusalem and protecting the Jews within its walls.

Seven hundred frustrated Arabs turned toward Hebron chanting, "Kill the Jews." For the next two days, they went door-to-door pillaging, raping, and decapitating Jews. Sixty-seven Jews were killed, and the bodies of all but ten of those were burned in a mass grave (flagrantly defying Jewish burial practices).[4]

But many of the "friends" in Hebron, who had lived in harmony for centuries, would not be intimidated. As many as 20 Muslim families hid their Jewish neighbors, refusing to let the mob in their homes.

> We sat silently in the sealed house and Abu-Shaker reported what was happening...The rioters had arrived. We heard them growling cries of murder...We also heard the voice of Abu-Shaker: "Get out of here! You won't enter here! You won't enter here!" They pushed him. He was old, maybe 75 years old, but he had a strong body. He struggled. He lay in front of the entrance to the home, by the door, and cried out. "Only over my dead body will you pass through here! Over my corpse!" One rioter wielded his knife over Abu-Shaker and yelled. "I will kill you, traitor!" The knife struck him. Abu-Shaker's leg was cut. His blood was spilt. He did not emit any groans of pain. He did not shout, he only said, "Go and cut! I am not moving!" The rioters consulted with each other; there was a moment of silence. Later we heard them leaving. We knew we had been saved. We wanted to bring our savior inside and bandage his wound and thank him. He refused and said that others might arrive and that his task has not ended yet.[5]

These Muslim heroes, one can argue, could be included with the Righteous among the Nations. They hid, defended, and protected their neighbors just as some Gentiles did during the Holocaust (see chapter 10).

Hearing this story, my father turned to me and whispered, "Did you know about this?" I did not. I had spent years studying the Palestinian–Israeli struggle, but never had I read about this event, which some scholars call Year Zero of the conflict.[6] After this massacre, which happened in other cities as well, the Jews started investing in military defenses against Arabs instead of trusting in their centuries of friendship.

Escalation of Tensions in British Mandated Palestine

Zionism—"the national movement for the return of the Jewish people to their homeland and the resumption of Jewish sovereignty in the Land of Israel"[7]—began in Europe in the late 1800s as a sort of political party. Their call to reclaim the historical land of Israel was not popular among most Jews, who were living comfortably and successfully around the world. But the events of the Holocaust changed that. After World War II, the Jewish population had dropped from 9.5 million to 3.5 million in Europe.[8] Support for Zionism grew as the people now believed they needed a place of their own where they could defend themselves after their European neighbors failed them.

Jews started moving into British Mandated Palestine, and tensions between them and the locals built. In 1947, the UN adopted a partition plan that was accepted by the Jews but rejected by the Arabs. The State of Israel declared its existence within the UN's allotted territory and announced its independence from the British Mandate on May 14, 1948. The next day, armies from Iraq, Egypt, Jordan, and Syria attacked. Over the next ten months, the State of Israel won 60 percent of the land designated to Palestine. At the signing of the war's armistice, it was agreed that Jordan would occupy the West Bank while Egypt administered the Gaza Strip.

Skirmishes between the nations popped up frequently, but in May of 1967, Egypt's president, Gamal Abdel Nasser announced he would be closing the Straits of Tiran to Israeli ships. Israel had previously indicated that such action would be considered a provocation to war, so Egypt sent troops to the border. On June 5, the war began, although it is unclear who fired first. Over the next six days, Israel won the Gaza Strip and the entire Sinai Peninsula from Egypt, the West Bank from Jordan, and the Golan Heights from Syria. Many Israelis believed this was a miracle from heaven, and Jewish settlers began moving into those new lands.

The next 20 years saw fewer skirmishes between the Palestinians and Jews living in the land. Palestinians were free to drive themselves to Israeli cities, with no checkpoints or just a handwave from a sleepy guard, but they were largely living in cramped refugee camps. The Camp David Accords were signed in 1978, in which Israel agreed to withdraw from the Sinai and give autonomy to the West Bank and Gaza over the following five years in exchange for full diplomacy with Egypt, but that never happened for many reasons.

On December 9, 1987, Palestinian uprisings began in the West Bank and Gaza. That day four Palestinians had been killed when an Israeli military truck collided with a passenger vehicle in the Gaza Strip. The protests, initially peaceful, spread to Jerusalem and the West Bank.

WHAT TO CALL THE "WEST BANK"?

The Jordanians named the area "West Bank" during their administration of it because the land was west of the Jordan River, and the nation of Jordan lies on the eastern bank. (Not particularly creative, those politicians!)

Tell someone you are going there, and you may accidentally make a political statement. No one likes that the Jordanians' name has been retained long after 1967, so each side has its own version. Israelis call it "Liberated Judaea and Samaria"; Palestinians and the international community call it the "Occupied Palestinian West Bank." Stay safe: All sides are fine with "Disputed Territories."

The Arab–Israeli Peace Process

The First Intifada officially ended on September 13, 1993, with the signing of the first Oslo Accords. Representatives of Israel and the Palestine Liberation Organization (PLO) agreed to a three-zone system that would allow for Palestinian self-governance after five years of transition. Israel did help the PLO become the Palestinian Authority as the future government, but nothing else happened. Israel kept building settlements, and Palestine kept attacking and inciting.

On September 28, 1995, the second Oslo Accords were signed that set up zones for the West Bank.

- **Zone A:** Israel completely pulls out of the Palestinian territories, settlements and all.

- **Zone B:** The Palestinian Authority has control of the area, but they are not sovereign. The PA is in charge of infrastructure—roads, utilities, education, health care—but not security.

- **Zone C:** The Israeli army is in full control of both infrastructure and security.

But Hebron was intentionally (and confusingly) left out of the Oslo agreements. When Israelis pulled out of the West Bank, they remained in Hebron. A special Hebron Protocol had to be drafted. In it, both parties agreed to create two districts in Hebron: H1 and H2. The Palestinians would control H1 and 80 percent of the city's population, while Israel would control H2 with the remaining 20 percent.

Today, Hebron is the largest metropolitan area in the West Bank. It contains one-third of the West Bank's population (over 700,000 people) and 1,400 factories. Hebron exports their high-quality leatherworks, finished stone (such as countertops), and handmade tiles widely.

SUBMISSIVE SILENCE

Neither Israelis nor Jews are allowed in H1, but unlike national passports that reveal nationality, there is no "religious passport" that reveals beliefs. In our group of 20, about half were non-Israeli Jews, and several of the men wore yarmulkes, the brimless caps worn by some Jews.

At the crossing, Eliyahu told the men they must remove their yarmulkes or cover them with ball caps to go into H1. The men started to protest, but this wasn't a law they could argue with. If they wanted to see H1 and the Muslim side of the Tomb of the Patriarchs, they had no choice. Our Palestinian guide was waiting for us on the other side because Eliyahu's American passport couldn't get him in as long as he wore his peiyot and tzitzit where all could see them. Plus, he knew everyone in the area after doing this tour for eight years.

Eliyahu warned us that the Palestinians staffing the crossing would ask the group as a whole, "Are any of you Jews?" and then, "What religion are you?" The Christians were encouraged to really speak up, and the Jews to stay silent. As half the group answered "correctly" for the whole, you could see the Palestinians rolling their eyes. "Yeah, right," they groaned to each other...in English.

Our next stop was Tel Hebron. The ancient city of Hebron has had some archaeological excavations since 1964, but not nearly as many as one would expect for the second most important city to Judaism and the fourth most important to Islam. Excavations of the Second Temple period did not begin until 2014, and the site is still in need of a comprehensive excavation that would give a complete picture of life on all parts of the tel during all periods.

Scholars have found that Hebron was a well-fortified city during parts of the Bronze Age (ca. 2500–2200 BCE and 1750–1550 BCE) and the Iron Age (ca. 1000–586 BCE). The Iron Age city was probably destroyed by the Babylonians in 586 BCE, as was Jerusalem and its temple. During the time when the second temple, Herod's temple, was in use in Jerusalem, Hebron appears to have been a well-organized city with homes, ritual baths, and industrial buildings. Four distinct civilizations have been found there, and the last version of the city was destroyed between the First and Second

Walking on an average sidewalk, we crossed over a recent excavation of Tel Hebron's Middle Bronze city wall.

Jewish Wars (ca. 132 CE). Hebron is mentioned in Byzantine, Islamic, Crusader, and Mamluk sources. The hill was finally abandoned during the Ottoman period, when nature took over and the tel became an olive grove.[9]

At a height of 3,000 feet above sea level, Hebron sits higher than any other biblical city.

At the very top of the tel is a low-ceilinged room, which tradition identifies as the tomb of David's great-grandmother, Ruth, and father, Jesse. Like so many burial sites in Israel, the historicity of this location is questionable. It was first mentioned as Jesse's burial place in the thirteenth century, and the ancient structure currently standing around the cave is from the Crusades.

Today it is common for Jews to visit the site on Shavuot, the Jewish holiday when worshipers read the Ten Commandments and the book of Ruth. Parts of the area now house a synagogue and a school for advanced Torah studies. The site is part of an army barracks, and a modern lookout tower stands on top of the Crusader ruins. It is still the highest point in Israel, so it still has the best views. What was good enough for King David and all subsequent occupiers is still good enough for the Israeli Defense Forces.

Palestine's 80 percent (H1)

By the time we climbed down from Tel Hebron, we were all ready to eat. Eliyahu took us to the border, we walked through showing our passports, and Mohammad introduced himself on the other side and quickly took us to the home of a local Palestinian family.

We walked down several steps into a partially underground space with a rustic cathedral ceiling that had been fully whitewashed inside. Sofas lined one side of the room, and on the other was built-in bench seating, a low table, and chairs. From behind a bright green door, the mother and daughter of the house brought us pita and hummus, traditional Mediterranean salads, and then a hot meal of roasted chicken and rice. They happily plunked two liters of warm Coca-Cola on the table, but those went mostly untouched. We all needed the bottles of water instead.

As we ate, Mohammad told us a bit about himself. He was in his midtwenties and had been born and raised in H1. He was a practicing Muslim, and like just about everyone else in his city, he had lost family and friends during the conflict with Israel. He was a relatively new guide for the Palestinian side of this tour, but he already had a reputation with the local Palestinian police. Later, as we walked through H1's modern market street, we were followed by an officer who silently dared Mohammad to say anything nice about Israel. Apparently, the leaders of H1 aren't thrilled that this tour exists and brings foreigners (and sometimes Jews) into their city; they had arrested Mohammad six times in the past.

After lunch, we walked to the market in Hebron's old city and met two shopkeepers. The owner of the first shop, whose family has woven linens and rugs for generations, ushered all the women to the back of his shop and sat us down on chairs and rugs. He told us how his family used to run several stores in that area, but that the Israeli occupation had caused them to close because of violence toward the owners and intimidation of the shoppers. He barely had enough customers to keep one store running, but he was trying to hang on as long as possible.

As we walked down to the next shop, Mohammad told us all to look up. Above our heads was a kind of chain-link ceiling. "See the Israeli flags? Settlers have moved in up there. They began throwing trash and rocks down on the market, and people were being seriously injured. We put up this net, but then they started dumping hot oil and other liquids down on us. We wanted to build a proper roof, but Israel said it would keep their soldiers from being able to keep the peace. So people stopped coming."

Next we went into Al-Qunaibi's Sesame Press. The proprietor again ushered everyone into the back of his labyrinthine store and invited the

ladies to sit. He explained to us how his family started this business during the Ottoman Empire. They pressed sesame seeds for oil and paste
using an ancient millstone, and those products are sold to food and
cosmetics manufacturers today. He also stocked his store with a collection of locally made goods, mostly glassware and ceramics. Those were
the work of the local women, he explained, many of whom were wid-
owed during the conflicts.

The last person Mohammad introduced to us was in charge of a
local organization called Human Rights Defenders. They supply video
cameras to H1 citizens, teach them how to use the equipment, then
post images of IDF violence against Palestinians. They don't have a
dedicated website, but you can learn a lot about their organization on
Facebook:

> Human Rights Defenders is a grass-roots, non-partisan
> Palestinian organisation working to support nonviolent
> popular resistance through popular direct action and doc-
> umentation of human rights violations committed by the
> Occupation.
>
> This project aims to document violations by the Israeli
> occupation through the distribution of cameras to Pales-
> tinian families in areas where violations occur on a contin-
> ual basis. Such documentation will expose how these Israeli
> practices violate international law.[10]

Not only are men routinely beaten and murdered, but families are
displaced from their ancestral homes. He told us how the Israeli army
uses their presence in H1 to increase the Jewish occupation of the city.
The Israeli Defense Force has a pattern. They enter a neighborhood
declaring they must build a military post on top of the Palestinian
homes. Once they have started the renovations, the Palestinians are
pushed out by a sort of "eminent domain," in which their properties
are seized but the owners are not paid. Then Israeli settlers move into
the newly renovated spaces.

CHOOSING SIDES

As Eliyahu was calling roll back at the hostel, I heard one woman say she would be staying in Hebron overnight. She was American and in her early twenties, I guessed.

As soon as we were on the ground in H2, she delighted in instigating the Jewish presenters. We all knew immediately that she was not on the tour to hear both sides of the conflict, but to disrupt Eliyahu's portion and to gain ammunition for her flagrant hatred of Israel from Mohammad.

She was a pain in H2, but her antics reached a new level in H1. After listening to the two shopkeepers tell us their stories, the group was given about five minutes to make purchases from them. (It wasn't enough time; we all wanted to buy much more from the men before Mohammad pushed us along.) Our group really stretched out along the market as everyone completed their transactions and then ran to catch Mohammad.

At our next stop about five minutes later, Mohammad did his usual head count; we were one person short. He panicked. He left the rest of the group alone in a dead-end alley while he went back to find her. After 30 minutes, he returned alone. "I called Abraham Tours, and they had her cell number. They reached her. When we got ready to leave the market, she decided to stay behind and skip the rest of the tour. Apparently, she wasn't going back to Jerusalem with the rest of you."

Having heard her tell Eliyahu about her plans that morning, several of us assumed this was probably the case. What she did was not only dangerous but extremely rude. Because of her, our time in the Jewish side of the Tomb of the Patriarchs would be cut to under ten minutes.

THE CAVE OF MACHPELAH

Genesis 23 tells the story of how Abraham legally acquired his first piece of land. His wife, Sarah, had died, and he needed a place to bury her and their descendants:

> Sarah lived one hundred and twenty-seven years; these were the years of the life of Sarah. So Sarah died in Kirjath Arba (that is, Hebron) in the land of Canaan, and Abraham came to mourn for Sarah and to weep for her.
>
> Then Abraham stood up from before his dead, and spoke to the sons of Heth, saying, "I am a foreigner and a visitor among you. Give me property for a burial place among you, that I may bury my dead out of my sight."
>
> And the sons of Heth answered Abraham, saying to him, "Hear us, my lord: You are a mighty prince among us; bury your dead in the choicest of our burial places. None of us will withhold from you his burial place, that you may bury your dead."
>
> Then Abraham stood up and bowed himself to the people of the land, the sons of Heth. And he spoke with them, saying, "If it is your wish that I bury my dead out of my sight, hear me, and meet with Ephron the son of Zohar for me, that he may give me the cave of Machpelah which he has, which is at the end of his field. Let him give it to me at the full price, as property for a burial place among you."
>
> …Ephron answered Abraham, saying to him, "My lord, listen to me; the land is worth four hundred shekels of silver. What is that between you and me? So bury your dead." And Abraham listened to Ephron; and Abraham weighed out the silver for Ephron which he had named in the hearing of the sons of Heth, four hundred shekels of silver, currency of the merchants.
>
> So the field of Ephron which was in Machpelah, which was before Mamre, the field and the cave which was in it,

and all the trees that were in the field, which were within all the surrounding borders, were deeded to Abraham as a possession in the presence of the sons of Heth, before all who went in at the gate of his city.

And after this, Abraham buried Sarah his wife in the cave of the field of Machpelah, before Mamre (that is, Hebron) in the land of Canaan. So the field and the cave that is in it were deeded to Abraham by the sons of Heth as property for a burial place (Genesis 23:1-9,14-20).

The locals didn't want to take Abraham's money at first, preferring to gift him the land, but they acquiesced and let him pay the 400 shekels. This was important to Abraham, so that the land could not be reclaimed from him in the future.

According to the Bible, the cave is the resting place of Sarah and Abraham (Genesis 23:19; 25:9), Isaac and Rebekah, and Jacob and Leah (Genesis 49:29-31). Jewish tradition adds the idea that inside the Cave of Machpelah is the ancient entrance to Eden, where Adam buried Eve and was later buried himself.

Herod modeled the synagogue on the temple's layout, so it is not only as old as the temple but it looks as Jerusalem's temple did during Jesus's lifetime.

The cave itself is underground, but no one has entered it since 1981. The building visitors enter was originally a rectangular structure constructed by King Herod to honor the fathers and mothers of the Jewish faith buried beneath it. The same building we soon entered has stood for over 2,000 years and has served its original purpose as a worship center for all that time. Certainly some renovations, repairs, and additions have been made, but when you look at the foundation stones of Herod's synagogue, you see them as they were in the first century. No wonder it is the only public building in the world that has remained in use for two millennia: Its stone walls are each six feet thick.

As Judea was conquered and reconquered from Roman times onward, Herod's building was reshaped for other People of the Book. The fourth-century Byzantine Christians turned the eastern part into a church, and 400 years later, the Arabs converted the church to a mosque. Then the twelfth-century Crusaders turned it back to a church, followed by the thirteenth-century Mamluks who turned it back into a mosque.

But the Mamluks did not stop with redecorating. They built minarets on top of Herod's walls, added buildings around them, and created rooms inside. Then they erected *cenotaphs*, large, rectangular monuments that honor the people buried far beneath the floor. In the center of the building are Abraham's and Sarah's, to the east are Isaac's and Rebekah's, and to the west are Jacob's and Leah's. In 1267, the Mamluks forbade Jews to enter the building.

JOSEPH OR ESAU?

The seventh cenotaph, which is under Muslim protection but is adjacent to the Jewish entrance, is a mystery. Muslim tradition states that Joseph was buried at the Cave of Machpelah in Hebron, not in Egypt as the Bible claims (Joshua 24:32), and this is his memorial. Jewish Midrash disagrees, claiming that Esau sold his right to be buried in the cave, he was decapitated by one of Joseph's grandsons during an argument over the property, and his head rolled into Isaac's dead lap where it remained.

Until the Six-Day War in 1967, the ban against Jews remained no matter the empire. Jewish worshipers were allowed to approach the building up to the seventh step. They would touch the walls of the building and pray, much as they do at the Wailing Wall today. When Hebron surrendered to Israeli forces, the Jews installed a small synagogue under the mosque so both religions could worship there.

But on February 25, 1994, the delicate balance was destroyed. An American-Israeli army doctor entered the mosque when both Muslim Ramadan and Jewish Purim were being celebrated. He opened fire, killing 29 and wounding 125 Palestinian Muslims. Surviving Muslim worshipers then beat him to death. Jews and Palestinians attacked each other as news of the massacre spread, and the Israeli government responded by closing the Tomb of the Patriarchs for a week and confining all residents of Hebron to a rigid round-the-clock curfew. When the site was reopened, it had new rules: It would be divided down the middle (mosque in the east and synagogue in the west), each religion would have complete access to the entire building ten days per year (on their holiest days), and when holy days overlap, each religion will get the whole building for 12 hours.[11]

Today, the dividing line between H1 and H2 literally runs down the middle of the Tomb of the Patriarchs, bisecting not only the building but also the patriarchs themselves. The Muslims get Isaac and Rebekah, and the Jews get Jacob and Leah. But poor Abraham and Sarah are split in two: heads in the mosque and feet in the synagogue (that is, if their bodies were really entombed there!). Solomon would not be pleased (1 Kings 3:16-28).

THE RIDE BACK TO JERUSALEM

After seven hours walking up and down hills in long pants, long sleeves, and (for the ladies) pashminas, we were all ready to board an air-conditioned bus. Standing at the stop just below the synagogue, members of our group took turns filling our water bottles at a public fountain. The last bus to Jerusalem was almost 20 minutes late, and by the time it arrived and we were rehydrated, a lot of other tourists had joined us. I noticed a particularly large family of Hasidic Jews—there were three generations at least—in addition to other tourists who had found their own ways to the Tomb of the Patriarchs that day.

Before the bus had stopped, a mob was at its door. Everyone was pushing, so the four of us hung back a bit (like the polite Southerners we are!), waiting for the chaos to calm. My mother had managed to slip onto the bus in the middle of the Hasidic family, but David, my father, and I were the last three people to enter it. I was still looking for a seat when the bus lurched forward, nearly throwing me to the floor. Next to me was the last open seat on the bus. It was a window seat, and a fourteenish Hasidic boy was in the aisle seat actively ignoring me. Thanks to nearly being thrown through the windshield seconds earlier, I didn't take the time to assess the situation. There was one seat. I needed to sit in it. I firmly but politely asked the boy to move over to the window.

He went white as a sheet, and I instantly realized what I had done. There I was, a red-haired female non-family-member foreigner, without her husband and head uncovered, instigating a conversation with a male Hasidic teenager. He looked as if I had asked him to come join me in a house of ill repute. He was terrified. Wordlessly, he tried to get the attention of someone behind him, and I looked back to see his parents giving me the dirtiest of looks.

All of this happened so fast that my father and David were not yet settled in their front-row seats. I yelled to David, "Hey, can you come sit here?" He figured out what was happening a lot faster than I had, and came back to trade positions with me. In the commotion, the Hasidic family played their own musical chairs with the people around them. My mother ended up sitting next to the grandfather (who manspread all the way back, she noted), and David got a seat with a Muslim Moroccan tourist who had been with our group. My dad and I were in the front row.

DAVID'S SEAT BUDDY

David would later tell the three of us that the ride home was the highlight of his day. He sat next to Aamir, who had come to Israel hoping to learn why there was so much hatred between Palestine and Israel.

Aamir was a Muslim from Morocco. He confirmed to David something that Eliyahu had told us that morning: Morocco is the only Arab country where observant Jews can walk freely. He described a society that sounded a lot like Ottoman Hebron: Muslims and Jews live, work, and play together, alongside Christians and atheists. It was unfathomable to him that people would not get along because they followed different religions.

He learned what we all had: Religious arguments over the land may have started the conflict, but it is now fueled by memories of past offenses. That is how the Gaza car accident launched the First Intifada. No Palestinian could imagine an Israeli "accidentally" hurting one of them. Where there is hate and hurt, there is no room for grace.

My family missed the end of the tour; Eliyahu lectured to the back half of the bus where everyone else had sat, and we had no hope of hearing him. So my dad and I compared notes about the day as we sped back to Jerusalem.

"Thank you for suggesting this. It has been the highlight of the trip," he said.

"I'm so glad to hear you say that. I was really worried that everyone would be mad at me for spending a whole day in one city, especially if something had gone wrong or you just hated it," I confessed.

"What did you think about it?"

I gave him my raw first impressions. "I came in to today expecting that by the time we left Hebron, I would be really judgmental of Israel. I've said for a long time that I don't think there is a solution to the Israeli–Palestinian crisis as long as humans are involved. Today reinforced that thought, but not for the reasons I expected.

"I loved how Eliyahu teased that this is the 'Competing Victimology Tour.' Both he and Mohammad walked us around and told us about the horrific things each side has done to the other. But I don't see one of them as the victim and the other as the aggressor, as I thought I would. They are both guilty of both.

"Eliyahu was factual. He wasn't afraid to say, 'Yeah, Israel shouldn't have done this.' He told us the good, bad, and ugly. Mohammad and his guests were overtly persuasive. They left out the unflattering facts about the Palestinians and would never admit any wrongdoing on their part. They seem to be consumed by their passionate hatred of Israel—we could feel that sometimes. I'm left wondering if what we saw and heard in H1 represents the citizens' thoughts and feelings, or if Mohammad and his friends are propagandists more concerned with getting international sympathies than having the interfaith dialogue they claim to promote."

My dad agreed, "If either side is driven by passionate hatred, then peace is unattainable."

CHAPTER 9

JUST JERUSALEM

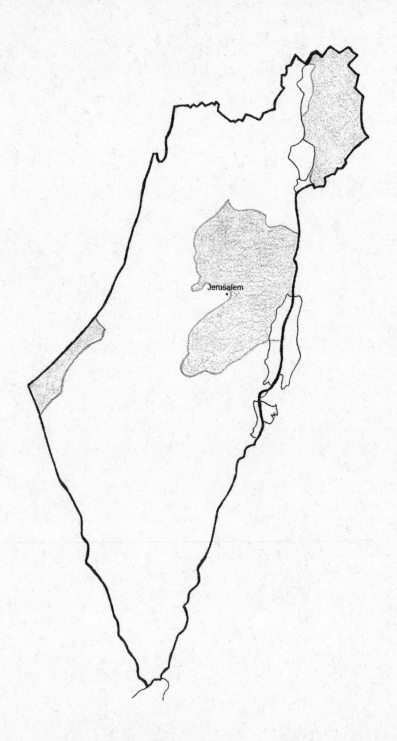

Jerusalem

Jerusalem lies at the very center—both literally and figuratively—of the Palestinian–Israeli conflict. As the seat of David's United Monarchy and home of Solomon's temple, it is the number-one-most-important city in Judaism. As the place from which Mohammad is said to have ascended into heaven, it is the number-three-most-important city in Islam. Both religions (as well as Christianity) encourage pilgrimages to the city and have fought to control it for centuries.

According to archaeologists, the first people to settle in what would become Jerusalem arrived around 3500 BCE. The settlement grew into a city as people built houses (ca. 2500 BCE), fortified the area (ca. 1800 BCE), and began trading with Egypt (ca. 1400 BCE). The true natives of Jerusalem were conquered ca. 1200 BCE by the Jebusites, a specific tribe of Canaan. From there, the archaeological and biblical records largely agree:

- **1000 BCE** David conquers Jerusalem and declares it Israel's capital city. Solomon builds the first temple there.

- **701 BCE** The Assyrians attempt to conquer Jerusalem, but they accept a tribute instead.

- **586 BCE** The Babylonians capture and destroy Jerusalem.

- **539 BCE**   The Persians conquer the Babylonians, which leads to the Jews' return.

- **425 BCE**   Nehemiah finishes the second temple.

- **332 BCE**   Rome conquers the region, allowing some self-governance by the Jews.

- **70 CE**   Rome destroys Jerusalem in response to Jewish rebellions.

The next big shift in Jerusalem's status came with the arrival of Christianity. In 313 CE, Roman Emperor Constantine officially outlawed the persecution of Christians within the empire with his Edict of Milan. He then sent his mother, Helena, to Israel to identify relics and sites holy to Christians. The Church of the Holy Sepulchre, which covers one of Jesus's supposed tombs, was completed in 335 CE and is the hallmark of her work.

SAINT HELENA

In 326 CE, Emperor Constantine's mother went to the Holy Land searching for sacred sites and relics. Helena had only been a Christian herself for about ten years at that point, but her work on behalf of the Christian faith changed the practices of the church. Tradition holds that she identified the places of Jesus's birth, burial, and ascension, and on those sites she commissioned churches.[1]

Near Jesus's tomb was a cistern containing three crosses and a sign that read *Jesus Nazaranus Rex Iudaeorum* (Jesus of Nazareth, King of the Judaeans). To identify which was Jesus's cross, she brought a terminally ill woman to the site and had her touch the crosses. The third one healed her and was declared the "true cross."[2]

Almost three centuries would pass before wars returned to Jerusalem:

- **614 CE**   The Neo-Persians capture Jerusalem.

- **629 CE**   The Byzantine Christians capture Jerusalem.

- **638 CE**   Muslim occupation of Jerusalem begins.

- **691 CE**   The Dome of the Rock is built over the ruins of the Jews' second temple.

- **1099 CE**   Christian Crusaders capture Jerusalem.

- **1187 CE**   Saladin captures Jerusalem, and Muslim empires hold it until the modern era (excepting two brief periods of Christian Crusader occupation).

- **1917 CE**   The British capture Jerusalem from the Muslim Ottoman Empire during World War I.

- **1948 CE**   The State of Israel declares independence from the British, and the Arab wars begin. An international coalition divides Jerusalem between Israel and Jordan.

- **1967 CE**   The State of Israel captures the Jordanian part of Jerusalem (including the Old City and East Jerusalem).

Historically, the nation who won Jerusalem (or any city anywhere on Earth) in war went on to rule it. Israelites took it from Canaanites, pagans took it from Jews, Muslims took it from Christians who took it from Muslims who took it from Christians; and always, to the victor went the spoils. But the rules of war changed with the formation of the United Nations in 1945. While Israel argued that they had rightfully won East Jerusalem from Jordan in 1967 during the Six-Day War, the international community told them they could not keep it. That formerly Jordanian territory was earmarked for the Palestinians, who had been displaced since 1948.

The verbal struggle for Jerusalem continues to this day. Israel says that they were the first to rule it (in 1000 BCE), and that they won it back fair and square in 1967. Palestine responds by saying that they have ruled it the longest (roughly 800 years), and that the UN says Israel can't have it.

That is a massive oversimplification, but it explains why each side has two good reasons to believe Jerusalem should be theirs. Unfortunately, there is no overlap in the criteria for the arguments and no agreement on their levels of importance. For the State of Israel, Jerusalem's status is primarily about who got there first.

CITY OF DAVID

The morning we were to tour the City of David, my family and I had trouble getting a taxi to take us to the other side of the Old City. We had already been in Jerusalem for a few days, so we had a good idea of how much that short ride should cost. The first taxi driver told us the fee would be triple what we expected. We were tight on time, and I just wasn't in the mood to haggle. I'm sure I made a face as I said no, turning on my heels toward a van just behind him.

He started a back-and-forth with my dad as I agreed to a lower fare with the other driver, and David and my mom started to follow me. The first driver piped up, "What will you pay? What will you pay?" and I told him our target price. He begrudgingly agreed.

What should have been a five-minute ride turned into thirty, and I started to realize why his first quote was so high: traffic. It was morning rush hour in Israel's capital, and countless tour buses were ascending to the Old City. As we crawled around Jerusalem's ancient walls, my family decided it would be faster to walk. We hopped out near the Dung Gate, where my father overtipped him for the trouble, and we could see lyre-shaped signs that read City of David in shiny gold letters. We would be taking Israel's official tour of the site, which was very well produced.

Thank goodness I had purchased our tickets ahead of time! I skipped that long line at the visitor center and walked right up to a volunteer who handed me four gold paper wristbands in exchange for my printed confirmations. A loudspeaker soon called all the English speakers to one area where our guide checked our bands and led us to covered benches.

Tina, our guide, started by surveying our group. We were mostly families, about 40 percent under the age of ten, and almost entirely American. Maybe half of us were Jewish, and our knowledge of biblical history ranged from not much to rabbi worthy. Our family fell somewhere in the middle. She handed each person a pair of 3D glasses and walked us into, as the website says, "an impressive hall built in the style of a fancy guest house of the Israelite period of the Davidic rule." Forty-nine velvet chairs were steeply tiered so everyone had a good view of the 16-minute-long film.

The first 15 minutes were fantastic. Truly. The film was obviously designed for all age groups, so the moderator was a bit cartoonish, but the information was solid. In a few minutes, we learned how tels develop over millennia of occupation, what has been found at the City of David, and what the Hebrew Bible indicates may be waiting in the dirt. Three-dimensional, full-color reconstructions then project the City of David as it would have looked in the first millennium BCE after David and Solomon built the palace complex at the top of the hill, and then in the 800s BCE when Hezekiah dug the city's cisterns. We even "toured" Solomon's temple, which would have been in today's Old City and not the City of David, and marveled at the high ceilings, gilded walls, and veiled holy of holies.

The Temple Mount, as viewed from the highest point of the City of David.

But in the last minute of the film, we learned this official tour was going to be neither unbiased nor fact-driven. It would be patriotic instead. The narrator stated that all of the discoveries at the City of David prove the modern State of Israel is the rightful and only inheritor of the land. Everything we had seen and would see on the tour was guaranteed to have us walking away from the site in full agreement. As we waited to exit the small theater, all four of us noted that out-of-place and wholly unnecessary final minute and prepared to exercise some Hebron-level discernment.

The group walked up to the highest point of the City of David. Tina pointed out the good breezes and glorious views of the Kidron Valley. It would have been hard to attack and easy to defend in the ancient world, she correctly told us. As we all stood on a viewing platform taking pictures and trying to imagine ourselves in a tenth-century, less-developed countryside, we heard loud, echoing pops.

The sound terrified several people, but Tina reassured us. "It's okay, it's okay. That happens every day. The Palestinians in East Jerusalem watch and wait for our tour groups to come up here, and then they shoot off fireworks. They are trying to get your attention and protesting Israel's occupation of the City of David." It was annoying and made it hard to hear Tina, but she was right. No harm was done.

Next up was the part I had most anticipated: a tour of the ongoing excavations at the City of David just south of the Temple Mount. I have long been a fan of Eilat Mazar, the director of those excavations. Archaeology is in her family's blood—her grandfather, Benjamin Mazar, was digging in Israel when it was still under the British Mandate, and her cousin, Amihai Mazar, appeared on every single archaeology exam I took at Harvard for his work at several Israeli sites. She is controversial in the academic community. Dr. Mazar publishes her findings quickly and is happy to "break a story" in more popular sources such as *Biblical Archaeology Review* instead of scholarly journals, often before other scholars have weighed in on her interpretations. Those interpretations tend to support traditional views of the Bible and, as we were about to learn, parts of her work are used to support the State of Israel's political narrative.

Excavation of the City of David happens beneath buildings currently in use today. Engineers must support the upper layers before digging occurs.

We moved down from the viewing platform, along an elevated walkway, and underneath the foundations of modern buildings. There was the Large Stone Structure that Tina dated to the time of David. "You are standing in the remains of King David's palace," she told us. "All around these very thick stone walls were found fine pottery and tools that would only have belonged to upper-class citizens of Jerusalem, such as the royal family. And look at this capital," she said as she pointed to the reconstruction of the top of a stone column that looked like a palm tree. "Based on the design, this could only have come from the tenth century BCE." Most in our group nodded in amazed agreement, but I knew of some scholars who dated that design as late as the second century BCE.

As we moved to our next stop, the City of David's vast underground water system, our group stretched out. David, my parents, and I kept up with Tina, but almost everyone else lagged behind taking pictures and helping the youngest members of their families. As we waited for everyone to catch up, Tina and I chatted. She was from Chicago but had lived in Israel for the last 20 years. She had been a tour guide for most of that time, but the City of David was by far her favorite job. She firmly believed the Large Stone Structure was David's palace. After telling her why I had been in Israel for the past few weeks, she asked me, "Do you think that is David's palace?"

I was honest. "I want to believe that it was. The information, as you've presented it, leaves little doubt that David put his palace here, in what would be the shadow of Solomon's temple. But we are only hearing the evidence that supports the theory. Before I raise my hand and agree that yes, this was definitely the center of the United Kingdom, I would want to see all of the excavation reports. I would want to consider the finds apart from the Bible. I love it when archaeology stands alone and then just happens to agree with Scripture. But I am dubious when people set out to find any artifacts described in the Bible and then do just that."

Tina really thought about what I said and then nodded. Behind her very scripted tour, I suspect that she agreed with me, though she could never say so. We talked on and off as we waited for the group to gather at each stop. She offered to introduce me to the on-site director of the dig (sadly, not Eilat Mazar herself), and asked me to lead the group through Hezekiah's Tunnel.

After touring the dry underground portions of the City of David's water system, the group had to part ways. "If you are going to get wet, stop here and change your shoes. When everyone is ready, follow Amanda." (Amanda had no clue where she was going, but Tina promised me it was impossible to get lost. There was only one way through the tunnel.) "If you don't want to get wet, then follow me. We are going to go up and walk through the older Canaanite tunnels. When you come out at the pool of Siloam, walk up the stairs, and you'll see me waiting for you."

I clicked on the tiny flashlight I'd asked David to bring with him from home and entered the pitch-black cave as my family followed Tina. The water was moving quickly, and if it had been deeper than my ankles at the mouth of the tunnel or if I hadn't been wearing water shoes, then I might have slipped. I thought about that water. In 2 Kings 20 and 2 Chronicles 32, the writers explain that King Hezekiah dammed the Gihon Spring, dug out the Siloam Pool, and carved this tunnel connecting the two. It was there to provide water to the city in times of siege, and Jerusalem would go on to face such a siege during his reign. As I continued through the sometimes-tight, sometimes-wide space, I found myself getting a bit chilly. I could feel that the water was crisp and clear, and it was rising to my knees. Nowhere in the tunnel were there rodents or bugs; I wanted to scoop up a handful and drink. Behind me a child did just that, and his father's angry correction echoed around us all.

I paused to wait for them and the following families to regroup and really looked at the walls around me. Most of the original plasterwork was in place, and some tool marks left in the underlying bedrock by the eighth-century BCE masons were still apparent. Just ahead was an ancient inscription describing how, in that place, the two teams who dug the tunnel met in the middle of the mountain to connect the spring and the pool.

It took about 20 minutes to walk the length of the tunnel. The sun was blindingly bright at the other side, but the children didn't seem to notice. Each and every one emerged from the rock and jumped into in the deeper, wider, and open waters of the Siloam Pool—where Jesus had healed a blind man under that same blazing sun 2,000 years earlier (John 9:1-11).

FLIRTY FRIENDLY FIRE

Before my first trip to Israel in 2004, 22-year-old me made a promise to my husband and my parents: I would not go to Jerusalem. My entire family was scared for my safety, and I was willing to make the sacrifice if it gave them peace of mind.

My friends thought I was crazy. Every Friday at Ashkelon, as we sat on upside-down buckets washing our day's pottery finds and discussing plans for that Shabbat (our only day off each week), they would ask me, "Why don't you just come with us? Your family will never know." For four weeks I gave the same unsatisfactory-to-them answer: "I promised I wouldn't go, so I won't go." But on Thursday of week five, in two separate conversations that they insist they did not coordinate, David and my mother each said, "You can't be in Israel and not visit Jerusalem. Go."

By Shabbat number five, most people were done with Jerusalem and exploring other cities, but my beloved roommates rented a car and took me on a whirlwind 12-hour tour of the non-Jewish parts of Jerusalem (because just about everything is closed in the Jewish Quarter on Saturdays). We knew that we wouldn't be able to approach the Western Wall—it was reserved for observant Jews on Shabbat—so we paused and admired it from a distance on our way to visit the Muslim sites above it.

A few months earlier, the old earthen rampart that non-Muslims had walked to the top of Haram al-Sharif had collapsed. The local government had hurriedly built a temporary wooden bridge for tourists,[3] and we slowly climbed the long line of still-green boards. At the top was an Israeli checkpoint, staffed by four bored soldiers, who were maybe 18 years old. "It's Shabbat. You can't go up there," one said. The guys kind of laughed and looked like they wanted to have a conversation with us, and one just had to show off. He took out his machine gun, twirled it in front of him...and dropped it. Bang! His friends started berating him, and since we couldn't be sure if that was a bullet or a blank, my also-newlywed roommates and I got out of there.

TEMPLE MOUNT AND NOBLE SANCTUARY

My family and I left the City of David and crossed the street just where we'd abandoned our taxi three hours earlier. We fought automobiles and crowds as we entered through the Dung Gate and into the Old City, mere yards from the Temple Mount and the Muslim holy sites above it.

We walked toward the western wall of this giant platform, where observant Jews pray regularly and slip written prayers into the cracks of an ancient limestone foundation. This was not the wall of either Solomon's or Nehemiah's temple, as some mistakenly believe. It is the remains of a 2,000-year-old retaining wall built and backfilled by Herod to enlarge and protect the space surrounding Nehemiah's temple. That temple was destroyed by the Romans in 70 CE, but they left the Temple Mount in place.

Today the platform stands 67 feet above the heads of those who pray there and has an area the size of roughly 24 American football fields. Muslims call the platform the Noble Sanctuary, and there they built the Al-Aqsa Mosque and Dome of the Rock upon it in the seventh century CE to honor Muhammad's Night Journey and ascension. It is an active pilgrimage and tourist destination for people of all faiths (although only Muslims are allowed to pray there), protected by the Israeli government but administered by a local civil Islamic body.

In truth, no one is really happy with a status quo that strives to preserve Muslim holy sites on the Jews' most important 37 acres in the world. Muslims want total control of the area, and many Jews (and Christians) want to destroy the Muslim buildings and construct a new, third temple that many argue would herald their coming Messiah. Short of that, Israelis want to know more about the Temple Mount. They want to excavate below the Islamic levels and find physical evidence of both Solomon's and Nehemiah's temples.[4] But such activities could literally undermine the Noble Sanctuary.

Israeli excavations have been done around the Temple Mount since the Old City became part of Israel in 1967, specifically near the southern and western walls. A particularly contentious 20-year project was completed in 1996. The 900-foot-long Western Wall Tunnel was trenched along the foundation of the Temple Mount, revealing many artifacts and building styles.[5] Many Muslims claim the tunnels are weakening the foundations of their Noble Sanctuary, causing cracks to appear in

Al-Aqsa Mosque and nearby Palestinian homes.[6] Israelis counter that the trenches contain structural supports (like those under the City of David) and do not go underneath the platform itself; they cite earthquakes and the Muslims' own building activities as the destabilizers.[7]

JERUSALEM'S MARKET

Leaving behind the Wailing Wall, my family ventured into the labyrinthine streets of the Old City, where we found shops, homes, and many religious sites. Every tourist wants to take home part of Jerusalem, and the market is the logical place to find just the right souvenir. But the savvy shopper must be cautious about what she chooses and with whom she interacts.

My mother is the savviest of savvy shoppers; much to her dismay, her daughter does not share that affinity. For days, as we had walked through the Old City on our way to one tour or another, I had never slowed down to let her browse. I was always laser focused on where we needed to be, and I knew from past experience that showing the least little bit of interest in an item could turn into a ten-minute-long haggle session that Western shoppers rarely won.

As I was navigating to one shop that my square mates had told me was particularly friendly to Western shoppers, my mom saw an item she could not resist. A long, narrow table just outside a shop door was set with hundreds of pomegranate-shaped vases. There were dozens of different designs and color combinations, all in the Hebron-ware style. Thinking of two friends back home, my mom picked one up and asked, "Do you think so-and-so would like this?"

Faster than I could pull her away, the shopkeeper was out his door and ushering her inside. "You like that? Come to the back of my shop! I have so many more! More sizes and designs." David and my father were in front of us, unaware of what had just happened. I yelled to my dad and motioned what had happened, screwed up my nerve, and ducked inside the shop myself. The shopkeeper already had her around a corner and squatting down in a dimly lit room where the same pottery was amassed on the floor. She selected two, but the shopkeeper countered, "Don't you like this one?"

Southern American graciousness is a major disadvantage in the market. "Well, I guess so. It's different than most of the others."

"Fifty shekels each!"

Oh, here we go. My mother played a good game. She pinched her face and said, "No, I think that's way too much."

"How much will you pay then?"

She looked at me for some idea. I threw out a low number. "Fifteen shekels."

He acted offended. "No! You know this is my job. I have a family to feed. They cost me much more than that. Thirty shekels!"

"Okay," I answered. "For both of them."

"No, no, thirty *each*." He puffed out his chest, taking up all the space between us and the exit.

I could just see my dad over his shoulder. "There you both are. Come on, let's go!"

The shopkeeper turned to him. "Oh, but don't you want to buy these for your lovely wife and daughter? Thirty shekels!"

"No, no, we have to go. I'm out of money. Come on, ladies."

Yes, way to go, Dad! I thought. *I'm ready to play the part of the weak woman this guy believes me to be and let my father save us!*

But the man turned back to me and took a step closer. We were not going to get out of there without money changing hands. "Forty shekels. For them both." The smile was gone from his voice.

"All I have is thirty. That is the best we can do."

"Okay, okay, you got me!" His smile returned. "Thirty shekels for both. I won't make any money on this, but you remember I gave you a great deal!"

As soon as he turned aside, my mother and I rushed out with our hastily wrapped package. "Did we get a good deal?" she asked me.

"Actually, I think we did. It isn't the handmade stuff like we will see at Balian's in East Jerusalem, but it was still made in Hebron. They are good souvenirs at half the price." But I was wrong. That night, as she unwrapped and admired the pretty pomegranates in her room, she saw that the orange-and-blue one—the one the shopkeeper pushed on her—was cracked.

THE WAY OF SUFFERING

As you walk through Old Jerusalem, you will occasionally notice tile signs in the walls reading "Via Dolorosa" in Arabic, Hebrew, and English (well, technically Latin). Along these streets, pilgrims follow the same path that eighteenth-century Roman Catholic tradition says Jesus walked from His trial to His crucifixion. The route is about half a mile long, with stops at 14 Stations of the Cross.

If you go to the first stop at Madrasa El-Omariya (a local elementary boys' school), you'll find maps of the entire route and a small museum. On that first day in Jerusalem before my family arrived, my square mate, Abby, and I saw a church group getting ready to walk the route as one of their congregants led the way with a wooden cross on his back. The last five stations—where Jesus was stripped naked, nailed to the cross, died on the cross, removed from the cross, and buried—are all inside the Church of the Holy Sepulchre.

JESUS'S THREE TOMBS

Spend a day in Jerusalem, and you can visit not one but *three* places where Jesus's body is thought to have lain for the three days before His resurrection. One is flashy, one is problematic, and one is peaceful.

Church of the Holy Sepulchre

No Christian's trip to Jerusalem would be complete without visiting the Church of the Holy Sepulchre. Completed in the fourth-century CE after Emperor Constantine's mother, Helena, identified the

Much of the church is glittering with gold and silver objects, colorful paintings, and bejeweled lamps. But as you enter the part of the building that was built by the Crusaders, you see the simple, poignant graffiti of thousands of Christian pilgrims.

site as the location of Jesus's three-day burial, this spot boasts the oldest tradition and the certification of six Christian traditions: the Greek Orthodox, Armenian Apostolic, Roman Catholic, and the Coptic, Ethiopian, and Syriac Orthodox churches. All six share the responsibilities of maintaining the massive building, which has been damaged and rebuilt several times, but territorial squabbles continue. To this day, one local Muslim family holds the 500-year-old cast-iron key to the church, and a second Muslim family opens and closes the building every day.[8]

It is easy to spend an entire day inside, visiting each denomination's own shrines and admiring artifacts such as the Stone of Unction (where they say Jesus's body was prepared for burial), the Rock of Calvary (on which Jesus was crucified), Jesus's prison cell, and of course, the Holy Sepulchre itself, where Jesus's body lay for three days.

Inside the domed rotunda of the Church of the Holy Sepulchre sits the Aedicule, a small, domed chapel that was built over the tomb itself, and the Angel's Stone, a fragment of the rock that closed the tomb. As we approached the Aedicule, my family debated: Did we really want to wait in line for over an hour just to get a glimpse of two rocks that may or may not have factored in Jesus's burial? Yes.

As we stood in the spiral line listening to countless languages, we had a lot of time to admire the architecture and decorations around

us. Above was a 12-pointed star, which the brochure said represented the 12 apostles Jesus sent into the world. Beside us were ten-foot-tall candlesticks burning brightly and velvet banners featuring a blue-eyed, European-looking Jesus. On the back side of the Aedicule was a small but elaborate Coptic Orthodox chapel.

Rounding the last corner of the Aedicule, we approached the opening to the tomb. Three Franciscans were monitoring the traffic. The first stood at the bottom of the steps and told us when to walk up, the second stood next to the doorway and told us when we could duck inside, and the third next to the tomb made sure no one snapped a photograph. This was a holy area, meant to be experienced, not Snapchatted.

This burial place of Jesus is in an elaborate building inside a more elaborate building.

Talpiot Tomb

About three and a half miles south of the Old City is East Talpiot, a Jewish settlement that has been part of the West Bank since 1973. It has two archaeological sites: an ancient aqueduct that watered the Temple Mount for 2,000 years, and a family tomb.

On Thursday, March 27, 1980, during the combined Christian

Easter and Jewish Passover weekend, a dynamite blast uncovered a tomb that had been carved out of the bedrock. Inside were ten ossuaries, six of which had names scratched into their limestone sides. One of those inscriptions read "Jesus son of Joseph." The other names were Mary, Mary Mara, Matthew, Jose (Joses), and Judah son of Jesus.[9]

THE JAMES OSSUARY

The plain, rectangular ossuaries at Talpiot resembled another contemporary and infamous burial box: the James Ossuary. In 2002, an antiquities collector in Israel revealed a first-century limestone box with the engraving, "James son of Joseph, brother of Jesus." It was immediately scrutinized as it was not found *in situ*; a grave robber had stolen it and sold it in the antiquities market, and then it was purchased in March 1976. The buyer who released the inscription's translation would soon be indicted on charges of forgery, as the international community questioned if "brother of Jesus" had been added to the ancient box recently. (He was acquitted, but the judge went on to say that the acquittal neither verified nor debunked the inscription. That question remains.[10])

Based on the physical similarities and ignoring the differences, the excavators from Talpiot have argued that the James Ossuary may have been stolen out of this family's tomb. Jesus's brother James is not otherwise represented in the family tomb, so if it could be proven that the James Ossuary came from there, then their theory that Talpiot was Jesus's family's resting place would be strengthened. Of course, this cannot be proven, and the burglary would have occurred at least four years before the tomb was discovered in the first place.

In 2007, Simcha Jacobovici, star of the A&E Network's television show *The Naked Archaeologist*, produced a documentary based on the discovery of these ossuaries. He interviewed several scholars on camera but then edited some of their comments to fit his new theory that Jesus's body only spent one night in Joseph of Arimathea's tomb. It was placed there quickly, but not permanently, due to the Sabbath laws. It was then transferred to His family's tomb in Talpiot, leaving Mary Magdalene to tell Peter and John, "They have taken away the Lord out of the tomb, and we do not know where they have laid Him," at the original burial site three days later (John 20:2). This documentary seemed to confirm Mary's worst fear that the grave had been robbed, while the Gospel writers had explained the absence with stories of Jesus's resurrection.

Understandably, the Christian community was not thrilled with Jacobovici's theory that undercuts the central belief that Jesus was bodily and not just spiritually resurrected. Most scholars who addressed the drama came out against the filmmakers and cited three major problems with the story: The six names were common in first-century Judaea, the family tomb of Jesus would more likely have been in Nazareth, and, most importantly, Jesus of Nazareth had no children![11]

Less than 200 feet away is another tomb buried deep beneath an apartment complex. Excavators used remote cameras to film everything inside, including eight untouched ossuaries, the earliest Christian symbol ever discovered (the Sign of Jonah), and the earliest testimony to the resurrection of Jesus—earlier even than the Gospel of Mark—a Greek inscription reading, "I, Divine Yahweh, raise up! Raise up!"[12]

Some scholars look at the objects found in Talpiot and conclude that Jesus's spirit did not return to His body. They would say that Jesus needed an ossuary because His flesh rotted off of His bones just as the flesh fell from His families' bones and will fall from the bones of every dead creature. Resurrection was figurative or maybe just symbolic to those scholars.

But I look at the data and see evidence of a faithful Christian community in the immediate wake of Jesus's crucifixion. Buried in these ossuaries were His followers, who may have been present at the crucifixion themselves. They believed in His work so deeply that maybe they named their children for Jesus, as we name our children after friends, family, or even heroes whom we hope our children will emulate. No doubt, these early Christians were touched by Jesus's life and message, so much so that they wanted later generations to see the Christian signs on their ossuaries and know in whom they had believed.

Garden Tomb

Just outside the walls of the Old City sits a more likely rival to the Church of the Holy Sepulchre's claim on Jesus's tomb, based on anecdotal evidence as opposed to a fourth-century tradition or archaeological finds.

After visiting the Garden of Gethsemane, my family made the poor decision to walk to the Garden Tomb. Waze told us it was a 25-minute walk, and we all felt up to it after resting in the Church of All Nations. Waze didn't tell us about the steep hill we'd be climbing along most of that route. (Learn from us: Look up from your phone once in a while, and you'll *see* the giant hill!) It took us about an hour to get there, with frequent stops to gasp for air and drain our water bottles.

The Garden Tomb is in the heart of the bustling city. Today its walls stand between a French seminary and East Jerusalem's central bus station, but in 1867, a local Jerusalemite thought it would be a great spot for farming. He began clearing the area so he could cultivate it and found a cave that was halfway filled with dirt and bones. The land was purchased in 1894 for 2,000 pounds sterling by the Garden Tomb Association, a group of Englishmen including the Anglican Archbishop of Canterbury. The men put up the walls, cleared the land, and planted the beautiful garden that remains there today.

We walked into the garden and were greeted by a thickly accented Texan. He, like all the other docents at the Garden Tomb, is a volunteer. People from all over the world sign up to work there for one 40-hour week each year. He handed us a pamphlet about the tomb in English and directed us to wait for Joe, who would show us around the site. "You're gonna love Joe," he said.

Joe was enthusiastic and maybe a bit too earnest about his work. He walked the four of us up onto a platform where we had a bird's-eye view of the garden and the bus station. In the distance was Skull Hill. He directed our attention to it and began his rapid-fire narration of the garden (in an even thicker Korean accent) with the help of some old, large, spiral-bound laminated photographs.

"Do you see that face in the cliff over there? That is called Skull Hill because it looks like a man's face. In Old Testament times, that was a rock quarry, but in Jesus's time it was where the Jewish officials held executions, especially stonings." He flipped open his homemade picture book. "Look at this picture of the cliff from 1900. See all those camels walking at the bottom? They are going to Damascus. Skull Hill was on a busy road, which is where the Romans liked to crucify criminals. Do you know that Jesus was crucified at 'a place of the skull'? It all fits, does it not?"

The Garden of Olives at Gethsemane contains the eight oldest olive trees in the world, which would have been present at Jesus's arrest. It is one of three sites the Franciscans maintain there, in addition to a church and a grotto commemorating Judas's betrayal and Jesus's arrest. The Garden Tomb lacks such strong historical connection to Jesus's story.

He turned us toward the garden. "And you know that the Bible says, 'In the place where He was crucified there was a garden, and in the garden a new tomb in which no one had yet been laid' (John 19:41). This is a garden in the place of the skull, is it not?" He walked us down into the garden and next to an excavated winepress. "You are standing under olive trees, but this used to be a vineyard. Only a rich man like Joseph of Arimathea could have afforded to make his own wine! So you see, this would have been a very good place to bury Jesus, would it not?" There our tour abruptly ended, as Joe directed us to walk through the surprisingly small garden to the tomb.

The tomb itself is carved out of limestone. The doorway is about four and a half feet tall and twenty-one inches wide. Stepping down about ten inches into the tomb, I could stand up in the space, but my husband and father could not. The ceiling is about six feet high, and the room is roughly ten feet by seven feet. There are places to lay three bodies on benches that were all about seven and a half feet long before the Byzantines made some alterations. Christian symbols are carved into the tomb's walls, evidencing its use by Byzantine Christians during the 300 years between Constantine's and the Muslims' control of Jerusalem.

Today, archaeologists believe that the tomb was actually carved during the Iron Age, when the kings of the United and Divided Monarchies were ruling Israel. They have found evidence that it was reused during the Byzantine period, but there is no evidence that it or any other cave in the area was used for first-century burials.[13]

As with so many of the sites we'd visited—in Israel and at home—we exited the Garden Tomb through a gift shop. There you are encouraged to leave a donation (there is no entrance fee) for the upkeep of the grounds and purchase some locally made items. I found a small watercolor of the streets of Jerusalem that now hangs in my office, and my mom bought some children's books for her grandnieces and -nephews.

The Garden Tomb is well worth the visit. It probably isn't where Jesus was buried, but it is a wonderful place for quiet reflection and worship without the glittering decorations and loud busyness that fill the Church of the Holy Sepulchre. They also have a cold-water drinking fountain, so tourists who are dumb enough to walk there from Gethsemane won't die of heatstroke.

JERUSALEM IN THE TWENTY-FIRST CENTURY

A little more than a block away sits a shop I have been raving about since 2004. Balian Armenian Ceramics is a third-generation, hand-painted pottery shop in East Jerusalem. You walk down a nondescript street with walls and doors built out to the sidewalk. When you find Balian's door, you must ring a bell. When the door opens, you find yourself in a tiny courtyard that is 20 degrees cooler. A tiled fountain is set into one wall, and the whole space is filled with thriving plant life.

Inside the next door, you see a long, wide hallway. To the right is the workspace, where Palestinian women sit at tables painting intricate designs onto tiles and vessels. At the end of the hall are large sample installations of murals, fountains, and pools—all made from the hand-painted tiles. To the left is the showroom and shop, where we spent over an hour admiring and selecting the pieces we would bring home. In 2004 (when it was still called Palestinian Pottery), I selected a tray with six tiles and a wooden frame. This trip I bought a small plate for myself and several vases to give as gifts.

As we were wandering around, the proprietor stuck his head in and greeted us. "Let me know when you need me; I don't like to stand over customers." That was Neshan. His grandfather immigrated to Jerusalem in 1919 when the British government requested that he and two other families come do repairs at the Dome of the Rock. He set up this shop in 1922, and the family kept it running through World War II and the Six-Day War.

The style of the pottery is so popular that it has been copied and the designs are mass produced. Walk through any city's market, and you'll see tables and windows filled with machine-made vases, bowls, plaques, and plates. Those items are commonly called Hebron pottery, as they were first created in Hebron in the 1970s. With a touch of annoyance, the Balian family will tell you just how inferior those products are when compared with theirs. Do yourself a favor and seek out the real stuff! You'll have a calm, cool shopping experience and avoid all the haggling.[14]

Starting to feel like pros, my family and I cut through the Old City (deftly avoiding charlatan shopkeepers) and walked back to our hotel. Going up Nablus Road, we noticed a lot of commotion ahead. A group of maybe 100 ultra-Orthodox Jews were blocking the road and the light-rail and chanting and carrying signs that read, "We will die and not be drafted."

All Israeli citizens, except the ultra-Orthodox Jews and Arab Israeli citizens, are required to serve two or three years in the army. For generations, the ultra-Orthodox were allowed to do religious studies instead of enter the army because of their specific religious convictions. But that changed in 2017 when Israel's Supreme Court ruled they would no longer be exempted. The court's reasoning was that the government was illegally favoring religious Jews over secular Jews, and that the composition of the army no longer matched the population's. Since the ruling, Jewish men have been arrested in their seminaries for dodging the draft.[15]

Protests such as that one, which seemed peaceful at the moment, have a habit of becoming violent when the Israel Defense Forces (IDF) arrive to remove the participants and get the city's transportation working again. But we managed to sidestep the protest and make it to our hotel safely. Everyone took a quick shower and dressed before we walked to our final Israeli dinner in West Jerusalem.

CHAPTER 10

LIVING HISTORY

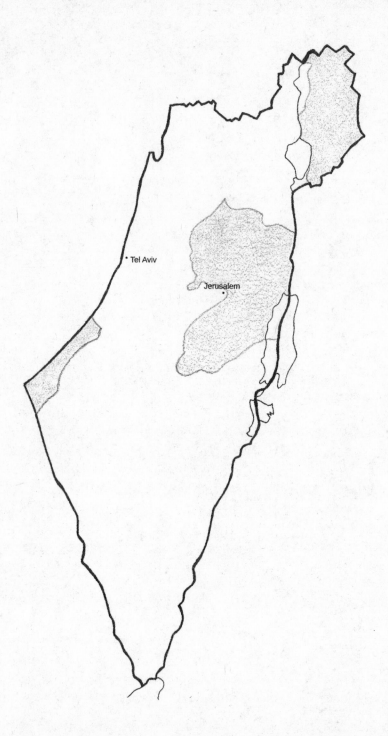

One more time I forced my family to hike up toward the Old City and then around into West Jerusalem. Pergamon Restaurant was just a mile from the hotel, and we could tell that a taxi wouldn't be any faster than hoofing it ourselves; we'd learned our lesson about Jerusalem's rush-hour traffic the previous morning.

As we neared the restaurant, the roads steepened, and we all slowed down. It was the first time we had been in part of the city that wasn't primarily touristy. Young adults were jumping off the buses on Jaffa Street and walking in every direction. Some ultra-Orthodox Jews were dodging cars with their bicycles, and more secular-looking citizens were ducking into small restaurants with friends. This vibrant area was near a couple of universities, and the businesses were just as shiny and trendy as you'd expect in any college town.

We had an early dinner reservation that night. We were the first group to be seated, but service was incredibly slow. Our server explained that the restaurant had only recently been tacked onto a popular bar. No one was eating yet (though that would change), but the bar was slammed with orders. The chef had been pulled over to help with the libations, so he sent out a free amuse-bouche to us as an apology.

We were there for three hours that night, so we got to know our server well. We asked her questions about this area where she worked and lived. What university is here? Is this an up-and-coming area?— that sort of thing. She answered casually, "Most everything around here is new or has been renovated. You know, because of that last café bombing." We were sitting one block from Café Hillel, where on September 9, 2003, a Hamas-backed terrorist walked up to the door and blew himself up, murdering six and wounding forty. This was during the Second Intifada, and it was the second suicide bombing to occur in Israel that day.[1]

> I don't know why I'm crying. I shouldn't even be moved by today—this is already my sixth attack...I can't take it anymore.
>
> —Sgt. Nurit Betzer, *a 20-year-old Israeli medic on scene at the café bombing*

Since that day in 2003, the terrorists' families have received stipends from the Palestinian Authority,[2] and sadly, state-sponsored terrorism is nothing new to the Jewish community. Even before the Jews were called Jews after their Babylonian exile in 586 BCE, their ancestors, the Israelites, were frequently targeted by outside, often more militarized nations. Throughout the Bible, they tangled with the Canaanites, Philistines, Egyptians, Assyrians, Babylonians, and Romans. Later, the Jews would be subject to Christian Byzantines and Crusaders, as well as several Muslim empires. Every time they were conquered, more Israelites and Jews were dispersed by the foreigners who came to rule their homeland. Then those displaced Jews faced anti-Semitism and persecution wherever they settled.

The modern State of Israel has made a point of recognizing all of their ancestors who were driven from the land with their many parks, memorials, and museums. My family bookended our trip to Israel with museums. We started with Israel's ancient history at the Eretz Israel

Throughout early-twentieth-century Europe, everyday items such as bronze ashtrays and coin plates, wooden pipes and cigarette holders, porcelain match holders and jugs, and long-nosed cane handles were too commonly decorated with grotesque Jewish stereotypes. The ideas that Jews were in league with the Devil, only cared about money, and were conspiring to take over the world were so common that some popular German children's books were based on those ideas. Society normalized racism against the Jews, paving the way to a mostly uncontested genocide.

Museum in Tel Aviv after everyone landed, and on our way out of Jerusalem—after that fabulous meal at Pergamon—we visited Yad Vashem, the World Holocaust Remembrance Center.

It is easy for archaeologists and historians to talk about the atrocities of ancient history as if they were the stuff of fiction. Destruction layers in the soil are always welcome finds because they are great for identifying the comings and goings of civilizations; we don't tend to think about the families who lost everything in those disasters. Any object that is found intact or almost intact gets special treatment, though little thought goes to the events that resulted in it being left behind. Even excavating an infant burial is more often met with excitement than sorrow by the volunteer chosen to do the job. These ancient deaths, no matter how real and how horrific, are too far in the past to elicit an emotional response from most observers. There are no photographs;

you can't look into the eyes of the victims. Your connection to the past is only as good as your imagination.

But the Holocaust is not ancient history, and Yad Vashem (which means "memorial and name") leaves little to the imagination. Throughout the one-and-a-half-hour audio tour, during which visitors are encouraged to stop frequently to view videos and read information posted inside the exhibit, *six million* becomes more than just a statistic that schoolchildren learn from their text books. The six million who died in the Holocaust are given names, lives, and voices.

The museum immerses visitors in early twentieth-century Europe and Asia, when Jews started out as valued members of those societies, were then segregated into ghettos, and finally were carried away to be murdered. Through objects stolen by the Nazis and recovered by the museum, you can see the photographs, documents, furniture, artwork, and games that once filled Jewish living rooms. You are sure to identify with something they, too, owned and valued, be it a shelf full of books, a child's drawing, a lovely necklace, or a chest of drawers like one your grandmother owned.

If you can't make it to a Holocaust Museum (there are several throughout the world), then spend some time on Yad Vashem's website. There you will find virtual exhibits featuring many of the same artifacts on display in the museum, videos from experts and survivors describing what the Holocaust was and how it happened, and educational tools for all ages.
https://www.yadvashem.org

Once you know the victims, the museum explains the genocide committed against them in sometimes-graphic details. Clothing from the concentration camps is on display, descriptions of and devices from mad-scientist medical experiments cover some walls, and everywhere are lists of names. People from this city or that country who were executed, and rarely, people on lists such as Schindler's who were saved. You witness evidence of all the ways the Jews were murdered—directly by bullets, beatings, and gas; and indirectly by disease, starvation, exhaustion, and suicide.

Pellets of Zyklon B converted to lethal hydrocyanic acid gas when they were exposed to water and warmth inside the Nazi gas chambers, where more than one million people were forced to inhale the gas and died.

In every circumstance of war, terrorism, and even genocide, God's people have inexplicably endured. Ten tribes may have been "lost" to the world when Assyria conquered the Northern Kingdom in 722 BCE, but the tribes of Judah and Benjamin hung on and kept their unique faith in one true God. The Nazis implemented a plan to murder every Jewish man, woman, and child, but a fraction survived Hitler's Final Solution. Arab nations have formally attacked the modern State of Israel en masse, but Israel has only ever gained territory in battles against them. And terrorist groups continue to murder Jews at bus stops and in coffee shops, but the Jews keep living their lives and worshiping their God.

Death and life regularly coexist in Jewish history, traditions, and society. Every Friday night in synagogues all over the world, Jews read

Germany wasn't the only nation that required Jews to identify themselves with sewn patches. Belgium, France, and the Netherlands issued these.

and remember the names of friends and family who died during that week in history. When they visit tombs, Jews will often leave behind a stone, noting the lasting presence of that person's life and the fact that the site has been visited by the living. Traditions such as these, which carry on the memories of people who have come and gone, is an ancient and central practice within Judaism. Therefore, commemorating the lives of those murdered during the Holocaust is the responsibility of the remnant who remained on this planet after World War II ended. At Yad Vashem, only four and a half million of the estimated six million murder victims have been identified, but space is reserved for the remaining undiscovered one and a half million.

For 4,000 years (more or less, depending on whom you ask), faith in their God and memory of their ancestors has helped the Israelites and Jews endure attacks from all people on Earth at one time or another. But how far will memory go?

It seems that anti-Semitism is returning. According to a study by the Anti-Defamation League in 2014, 1 in 4 people hold anti-Semitic attitudes worldwide[3]: "The chief idea behind new anti-Semitism today is the demonic image of the State of Israel and Zionism."[4] Based on the consistently anti-Israel resolutions that come from the United Nations, it seems that most foreign world leaders have decided among themselves that the State of Israel has no right to exist.

The world does have legitimate concerns; the State of Israel has an egregious record of crimes against Palestinians. In their understandable eagerness to secure safety for Jewish Israelis after the "recent" Holocaust and generations of conquest, some Jewish officials and citizens have acted inhumanely, making it easier for the world to characterize the entire country and all of its people as villains than to understand why Israelis feel constantly threatened by their neighbors. The international community is once again becoming comfortable with dehumanizing a specific group of people on the basis of half-truths in the news and a dwindling familiarity with history. It may be less noticeable in the US, where the ADL finds that less than ten percent of Americans are anti-Semitic, but consider that one-quarter of the earth's population is okay with hating people they've never met.[5]

I have long said that I don't believe there will be a solution to the Palestinian–Israeli conflict on "this side of heaven," mostly because humans are involved. Since before Abraham bought a burial cave in Hebron, wrongs have been committed against his descendants and by his descendants; history and the Bible itself bear that out. The Jews and Muslims who both count him as a patriarch have been perpetually unable to compromise because both groups see themselves as God's only right-worshiping children, as the only legitimate inheritors of the land, and as the most-victimized victims.

When humanity wants to take sides and fight wars, only perfect grace can stop the suffering. But none of us are capable of perfect anything. We try to make treaties and do better, but the memories of past wrongs remain, keeping us wary and fearful of each other. We must learn how to love each other. Love our families, love our neighbors, and love our enemies no matter who they are or what they (or their ancestors) have done. It is a tall order that requires an investment of precious time, but nothing of value comes quickly. Just ask the volunteer down in a hole moving dirt with a paintbrush.

In those places where we don't understand what is happening, in the world or in Scripture, we can't be afraid to dig! We should all be archaeologists, "digging" into history and Scripture and learning about each other's cultures. Remember that archaeology, at its core, is concerned with discovering who our ancestors were and how they lived. The tools and bowls left behind allow us to better identify with the people of Abraham's or David's or Jesus's times because they remind us that people have always had the same needs for water, food, shelter, clothing, and relationships that we all do today. Finding Noah's ark or

Moses's ark or Jesus's cup would be fun, but it wouldn't be instructive. They wouldn't teach us about God or each other.

As Genesis 3:19 reminds us, we all come from dirt and will one day return to it. So in this life—this space between creation and death— don't be afraid to get some dirt under your nails, behind your knees, or all over your shirt. Those stains, be they literal or figurative, that you get from engaging with God's planet and people will deepen your appreciation of the Creator and His creations.

NOTES

INTRODUCTION: MEET THE RED-HAIRED ARCHAEOLOGIST

1. Hershel Shanks, "Where Is the Tenth Century?" *Biblical Archaeology Review* 24, no. 2 (1998): 56-60.

2. Steve Weiner and Elisabetta Boaretto, "Microarchaeology at Tell eṣ-Ṣâfi/Gath, Area A," *Near Eastern Archaeology* 81, no. 1 (March 2018): 24-27.

CHAPTER 2: FIGHTING PHILISTINES ON THE MEDITERRANEAN SEA

1. Michal Feldman et al., "Ancient DNA sheds light on the genetic origins of early Iron Age Philistines," *Science Advances* 5, no. 7 (3 Jul 2019): 1, https://advances.sciencemag.org/content/5/7/eaax0061.

2. "About," *The Leon Levy Expedition to Ashkelon*, http://digashkelon.com/about.

3. "Moses Hears God While His Flock Loses Itself," *The Ten Commandments*, directed by Cecil B. DeMille (1956; Hollywood, CA: Paramount, 2017), Blu-ray Disc.

4. "Project Overview," *The Tell es-Safi/Gath Archaeological Project Official (and Unofficial) Weblog*, https://gath.wordpress.com/about/project-overview/.

5. Aren M. Maier, quoted in Amanda Borschel-Dan, "Colossal ancient structures found at Gath may explain origin of story of Goliath," *Times of Israel*, July 26, 2019, https://www.timesofisrael.com/colossal-ancient-structures-found-at-gath-may-explain-origin-of-story-of-goliath/.

6. Trude Dothan, "Ekron of the Philistines, Part I: Where They Came From, How They Settled Down and the Place They Worshiped In," *Biblical Archaeology Review* 16, no. 1 (1990): 26-31, 33-36, https://www.baslibrary.org/biblical-archaeology-review/16/1/2.

7. *Ashdod-Yam Archaeological Project* (blog), Institute of Archaeology at Tel Aviv University, https://archaeological.wixsite.com/ashdodyam.

8. Trude Dothan, "What We Know About the Philistines," *Biblical Archaeology Review* 8, no. 4 (July/August 1982): 20-44, https://www.baslibrary.org/biblical-archaeology-review/8/4/1.

9. "Gazans Struggle to Protect Antiquities Under Hamas Rule, Israeli Blockade," *Haaretz*, August 9, 2019, https://www.haaretz.com/archaeology/gazans-struggle-to-protect-antiquities-from-neglect-and-looting-1.7653856.

10. "Gaza's archaeological treasures at risk from war and neglect," *BBC News*, January 7, 2013, https://www.bbc.com/news/world-middle-east-20853440.

11. "An Ancient Canaanite Treasure in Gaza Was Leveled to the Ground by Hamas," *Haaretz*, October 8, 2017, https://www.haaretz.com/middle-east-news/palestinians/hamas-levels-ancient-canaanite-treasure-in-gaza-1.5455968.

12. Ann Gibbons, "Biblical Philistines—archenemies of ancient Israelites—hailed from Europe, DNA reveals," *Science* 365, no. 6448 (5 July 2019): 17, https://www.sciencemag.org/news/2019/07/biblical-philistines-archenemies-ancient-israelites-hailed-europe-dna-reveals; Kristin Romey, "Ancient DNA may reveal origin of the Philistines," *National Geographic* 170, no. 7 (3 July 2019): https://www.nationalgeographic.com/culture/2019/07/ancient-dna-reveal-philistine-origins/.

13. Benjamin Netanyahu (@netanyahu), Twitter, July 7, 2019, 7:08 a.m., https://twitter.com/netanyahu/status/1147824702360100864?lang= (emphasis added).

14. Feldman et al., "Ancient," https://advances.sciencemag.org/content/5/7/eaax0061/tab-pdf.

CHAPTER 3: DEATH AND LIFE IN NEGEV'S DUSTY DESERT

1. *Merriam-Webster's Collegiate Dictionary*, 11th ed. (2009), s.v. "desert."

2. "Negev Highlands," *Israel's Long-term Ecosystem Research Network*, November 20, 2018, http://lter-israel.org.il/index.php/portfolio-items/negev-highlands-ltser-platform/.

3. "Israel's Desert Agriculture," *Tourist Israel*, https://www.touristisrael.com/israels-desert-agriculture/10334/.

4. Seth J. Frantzman, Ruth Kark, "Bedouin Settlement in Late Ottoman and British Mandatory Palestine: Influence on the Cultural and Environmental Landscape, 1870–1948," British Society for Middle Eastern Studies, June 15, 2001, http://www.brismes.ac.uk/nmes/wp-content/uploads/2011/06/NMES2011FrantzmanKark.pdf; Kurt Goering, "Israel and the Bedouin of the Negev," *Journal of Palestine Studies* 9, no. 1 (Autumn 1979): 3-20, https://www.jstor.org/stable/2536316; "Behind the Headlines: The Bedouin in the Negev and the Begin Plan," Israeli Ministry of Foreign Affairs, November 4, 2013, https://mfa.gov.il/MFA/ForeignPolicy/Issues/Pages/The-Bedouin-in-the-Negev-and-the-Begin-Plan-4-Nov-2013.aspx.

5. Miriam Aharoni, Ze'ev Herzog, and Anson F. Rainey, "Arad—An Ancient Israelite Fortress with a Temple to Yahweh," *Biblical Archaeology Review* 13, no. 2 (1987): 16-35, https://www.baslibrary.org/biblical-archaeology-review/13/2/1.

6. Don Knebel, "Biblical History at Karnak Temple," *Bible History Daily*, September 3, 2019, https://www.biblicalarchaeology.org/uncategorized/biblical-history-at-karnak-temple/.

7. Aharoni et al, "Arad," https://www.baslibrary.org/biblical-archaeology-review/13/2/1.

8. David Ussishkin, "Answers at Lachish," *Biblical Archaeology Review* 5, no. 6 (November/December 1979): 16-38, https://www.baslibrary.org/biblical-archaeology-review/5/6/1.

9. "Tel Lachish Excavations," *Tracing Transformations in the Southern Levant* (blog), https://tracingtransformations.com/tel-lachish-excavations/.

10. Trent C. Butler, *Joshua*, Word Biblical Commentary, vol. 7 (Dallas: Word Books, 1984), 244-49.

11. Ze'ev Herzong, *Tel Beer Sheva National Park* (brochure), trans. Miriam Feinberg Vamosh (Israel Nature and Parks Authority, 2018).

12. "Horned Altar for Animal Sacrifice Unearthed at Beer-Sheva," *Biblical Archaeology Review* 1, no. 1 (1975): 1, 8-9, 15, https://www.baslibrary.org/biblical-archaeology-review/1/1/2.

CHAPTER 4: BOBBING IN WATER AND HIKING TO CAVES AT THE DEAD SEA

1. *Nova*, season 46, episode 7, "Saving the Dead Sea," produced by Paula S. Apsell, aired April 24, 2019, on PBS.

2. Ibid.

3. Ibid.

4. Kevin Connolly, "Dead Sea drying: A new low-point for Earth," *BBC News*, June 17, 2016, https://www.bbc.com/news/world-middle-east-36477284.

5. Yigael Yadin, *Masada: Herod's Fortress and the Zealots' Last Stand*, trans. Moshe Pearlman (New York: Random House, 1966).

6. Guy Stiebel and Boaz Gross, "Masada Shall Never Fail (to Surprise) Again," *Biblical Archaeology Review* 44, no. 5 (2018): 30-40, https://www.baslibrary.org/biblical-archaeology-review/44/5/2.

7. "World Heritage," United Nations Educational, Scientific and Cultural Organization (UNESCO), https://whc.unesco.org/en/about/.

8. "Meet En Gedi Nature Reserve," Israel Nature and Parks Authority, https://www.parks.org.il/en/reserve-park/en-gedi-nature-reserve/.

9. *Nova*, season 46, episode 7, "Saving the Dead Sea," produced by Paula S. Apsell, aired April 24, 2019, on PBS.

10. *Qumran National Park* (brochure), Israel Nature and Parks Authority Publishing, 2011.

11. Ben Zion Wacholder and Martin G. Abegg, eds., *Preliminary Edition of the Unpublished Dead Sea Scrolls—The Hebrew and Aramaic Texts from Cave Four* (Washington: Biblical Archaeology Society, 1991).

12. Martin Abegg, "Hershel's Crusade, No. 1: He Who Freed the Dead Sea Scrolls," *Biblical Archaeology Review* 44, no. 2 (2018): 24-28, https://www.baslibrary.org/biblical-archaeology-review/44/2/3.

13. Adam S. van der Woude, "Tracing the Evolution of the Hebrew Bible," *Bible Review* 11, no. 1 (1995): 42-45, https://www.baslibrary.org/bible-review/11/1/11.

CHAPTER 5: MEETING DISCIPLES AT THE SEA OF GALILEE

1. Heidi Schlumpf, "Who framed Mary Magdalene?" *U.S. Catholic* 65, no. 4 (April 2000): 12-16, http://www.uscatholic.org/articles/200806/who-framed-mary-magdalene-27585.

2. "About," Magdala, https://www.magdala.org/.

3. Jennifer Ristine, "Magdalena Institute," Magdala: Crossroads of Jewish and Christian History, https://www.magdala.org/visit/magdalena-institute/.

4. "Ten Top Discoveries," *Biblical Archaeology Review* 35, no. 4 (2009): 88-90.

5. "Capernaum," Israel Ministry of Foreign Affairs, March 7, 2000, https://mfa.gov.il/MFA/MFA -Archive/2000/Pages/Capernaum.aspx.

6. "Capernaum," Custodia Terra Sanctae, https://www.custodia.org/pt-pt/node/155496.

7. *The Lexham Bible Dictionary*, rev. ed. (Bellingham, WA: Lexham, 2016), s.v. "Gennesaret."

8. B. Cobbey Crisler, "The Acoustics and Crowd Capacity of Natural Theaters in Palestine," *The Biblical Archaeologist* 39, no. 4 (December 1976): 128-41.

9. *Encyclopaedia Britannica Online*, s.v. "Sea of Galilee," last modified April 29, 2019, https://www .britannica.com/place/Sea-of-Galilee.

CHAPTER 6: WINE, WAR, AND WALLS IN THE GOLAN HEIGHTS

1. "'World's oldest wine' found in 8,000-year-old jars in Georgia," *BBC News*, November 13, 2017, https://www.bbc.com/news/world-europe-41977709.

2. "Strata: Was This Noah's Winery?" *Biblical Archaeology Review* 37, no. 5 (2011): 20, https://www .baslibrary.org/biblical-archaeology-review/37/5/18.

3. "Travel: Israel," *Wine Enthusiast*, https://www.winemag.com/region/israel/.

4. Norma Franklin et al, "Have We Found Naboth's Vineyard at Jezreel?" *Biblical Archaeology Review* 43, no. 6 (2017): 49-54, https://www.biblicalarchaeology.org/magazine/have-we-found -naboths-vineyard-at-jezreel/.

5. "History of Israel Wines," Israel Wine Producers Association, http://iwpa.com/history.php.

6. "Our Team," *The Israel Wine Experience*, http://www.israelwinexp.com/more-about-us/our-team /oded-shoham/.

7. Blu Greenberg, "Keeping Kosher: Shopping for Kosher Food," *My Jewish Learning*, https://www .myjewishlearning.com/article/shopping-for-kosher-food/.

8. Jewish Telegraphic Agency, "Major department store in Japan bans wine from Golan Heights at special event," *Jerusalem Post*, June 4, 2018, https://www.jta.org/2018/06/04/israel/major-depar

tment-store-chain-japan-banned-wine-golan-heights-special-event; Rupert Millar, "Ontario Over-turns Israeli Wine Ban," *The Drinks Business*, July 14, 2017, https://www.thedrinksbusiness.com/2017/07/ontario-overturns-israeli-wine-ban/.

9. Jacey Fortin, "A Brief History of the Golan Heights, Claimed by Israel and Syria," *New York Times*, March 29, 2019, https://www.nytimes.com/2019/03/21/world/middleeast/golan-heights-israel.html.

10. Ben Hubbard, "The Golan Heights Was Once an Arab Rallying Cry. Not Anymore," *New York Times*, March 22, 2019, https://www.nytimes.com/2019/03/22/world/middleeast/golan-heights-israel-syria.html.

11. Lubna Omar, "I'm one of hundreds of archaeologists exiled from Syria who's mourning what the war is costing us," *The Conversation*, August 12, 2019, https://theconversation.com/im-one-of-hundreds-of-archaeologists-exiled-from-syria-whos-mourning-what-the-war-is-costing-us-116325.

12. "Cultural Heritage Initiatives," American Society of Oriental Research, http://www.asor.org/chi.

13. Michael D. Danti et al, "Special Report: Current Status of the Tell Ain Dara Temple," *ASOR Cultural Heritage Initiatives*, March 9, 2018, https://www.biblicalarchaeology.org/daily/news/special-report-current-status-tell-ain-dara-temple/.

14. *Tel Dan Nature Reserve* (brochure), Israel Nature and Parks Authority Publishing, 2018.

15. "Ten Top Discoveries," *Biblical Archaeology Review* 35, no. 4 (2009): 82-84, https://www.baslibrary.org/biblical-archaeology-review/35/4/15.

16. Thomas H. Maugh II, "Stone Tablet Offers 1st Physical Evidence of Biblical King David," *Los Angeles Times*, August 14, 1993, https://www.latimes.com/archives/la-xpm-1993-08-14-me-23862-story.html.

CHAPTER 7: ROLLING THROUGH GALILEE

1. Daniel M. Master, "Launching Excavations at Tel Shimron," *Biblical Archaeology Review* 44, no. 5 (2018): 56-60, https://www.baslibrary.org/biblical-archaeology-review/44/5/5.

2. Mario Martin, quoted in Megan Sauter, "Digging Deep at Tel Shimron: 5 Questions for the Directors of Tel Shimron," *Bible History Daily*, December 30, 2019, https://www.biblicalarchaeology.org/daily/archaeology-today/digging-deep-at-tel-shimron/.

3. Ken Dark, "Has Jesus' Nazareth House Been Found?" *Biblical Archaeology Review* 41, no. 2 (2015): 54-63.

4. Steve Mason, "O Little Town of…Nazareth?" *Bible Review* 16, no. 1 (2000): 32-39, 51-53; https://www.baslibrary.org/bible-review/16/1/11.

5. Inbal Samet, *Megiddo National Park* (brochure), trans. Miriam Feinberg Vamosh (Israel Nature and Parks Authority, n.d.); David E. Aune, *Revelation 6–16*, Word Biblical Commentary 52B (Dallas: Word, 1998), 898-99.

6. Israel Finkelstein and Neil Asher Silberman, *The Bible Unearthed: Archaeology's New Vision of Ancient Israel and the Origin of Its Sacred Texts* (New York: Free Press, 2002).

7. William G. Dever, "Hershel's Crusade, No. 2: For King and Country: Chronology and Minimalism," *Biblical Archaeology Review* 44, no. 2 (2018): 31-36, https://www.baslibrary.org/biblical-archaeology-review/44/2/4.

8. Mazar, Amihai, and John Camp. "Will Tel Rehov Save the United Monarchy?" *Biblical Archaeology Review* 26, no. 2 (2000): 38-40, 42-45, 47-48, 50-51, 75, https://www.baslibrary.org/biblical-archaeology-review/26/2/5.

CHAPTER 8: FRIEND AND FOE IN HEBRON

1. "Hebron Dual Narrative Tour," *Abraham Tours*, https://abrahamtours.com/tours/hebron-tour/.

2. Qur'an 2:105,109; 3:64,65,69-72,75; 5:15,19; 33:26; 57:29.

3. Anita Vitullo, "People Tied to Place: Strengthening Cultural Identity in Hebron's Old City," *Journal of Palestine Studies* 33, no. 1 (Fall 2003): 68-83.

4. Eliyahu McLean, "Hebron Dual Narrative Tour," August 14, 2019.

5. Malka Slonim, quoted in Edward Platt, *City of Abraham: History, Myth and Memory; A Journey through Hebron* (London: Picador, 2012), 88.

6. Hillel Cohen, *Year Zero of the Arab–Israeli Conflict 1929*, trans. Haim Watzman (Waltham, MA: Brandeis University Press, 2015).

7. American-Israeli Cooperative Enterprise, "Zionism: A Definition of Zionism," Jewish Virtual Library, https://www.jewishvirtuallibrary.org/a-definition-of-zionism.

8. United States Holocaust Memorial Museum, "Remaining Jewish Population of Europe in 1945," *Holocaust Encyclopedia*, https://encyclopedia.ushmm.org/content/en/article/remaining-jewish -population-of-europe-in-1945.

9. David Ben-Shlomo, "Hebron Still Jewish in Second Temple Times," *Biblical Archaeology Review* 43, no. 5 (2017): 32-39, 64, https://www.baslibrary.org/biblical-archaeology-review/43/5/3.

10. "Our Story," Human Rights Defenders, March 22, 2019, https://www.facebook.com/pg/Human -Rights-Defenders-727496507326993-تجمع المدافعين عن حقوق الانسان/about/.

11. "The Ibrahimi Mosque Massacre: 20 Years Later," Institute for Middle East Understanding, February 27, 2014, https://imeu.org/article/the-ibrahimi-mosque-massacre-20-years-later.

CHAPTER 9: JUST JERUSALEM

1. Fr. William Saunders, "Straight Answers: St. Helena and the True Cross," *Arlington Catholic Herald* 30, no. 37 (September 15, 2005): 8.

2. Ibid.

3. Barak Ravid and Nir Hasson, "PM Orders Removal of Wooden Ramp at Temple Mount, Following Pressure from Jordan," *Haaretz*, September 3, 2014, https://www.haaretz.com/ .premium-pm-orders-removal-of-wooden-ramp-at-temple-mount-1.5262985.

4. Leen Ritmeyer, "Locating the Original Temple Mount," *Biblical Archaeology Review* 18, no. 2 (1992):24,26,29,32-37,43-45,65,https://www.baslibrary.org/biblical-archaeology-review/18/2/1.

5. Dan Bahat, "Jerusalem Down Under: Tunneling Along Herod's Temple Mount Wall," *Biblical Archaeology Review* 21, no. 6 (1995): 30-35, 37-40, 42-47, https://www.baslibrary.org/biblical -archaeology-review/21/6/2.

6. Aness Suheil Barghoti, "Israeli excavations threaten Al-Aqsa Mosque: Experts; Israel refuses to allow access to UNESCO to examine holy sites in East Jerusalem," *Anadolu Agency*, August 8, 2019, https://www.aa.com.tr/en/middle-east/israeli-excavations-threaten-al-aqsa-mosque-experts /1552432.

7. Nir Hasson, "Jerusalem's Time Tunnels," *Haaretz*, April 24, 2011, https://www.haaretz.com /1.5003615.

8. Oren Liebermann, "Two Muslim families entrusted with care of holy Christian site for centuries," CNN, March 27, 2016, https://www.cnn.com/2016/03/26/middleeast/easter-muslim-keyholder /index.html.

9. James D. Tabor, *The Jesus Dynasty: The Hidden History of Jesus, His Royal Family, and the Birth of Christianity* (New York: Simon & Schuster, 2006), 319-31.

10. Hershel Shanks, "First Person: 'The Tomb of Jesus'—My Take," *Biblical Archaeology Review* 33, no. 4 (2007): 4, 72, https://www.baslibrary.org/biblical-archaeology-review/33/4/2.

11. Jodi Magness, "Has the Tomb of Jesus Been Discovered? 'Jesus Tomb' Controversy Erupts—Again," *Bible History Daily*, March 5, 2007, https://www.biblicalarchaeology.org/daily/archaeology-today/biblical-archaeology-topics/has-the-tomb-of-jesus-been-discovered/.

12. James D. Tabor, "The Talpiot 'Jesus' Tomb: What's the Latest?" (lecture, University of North Carolina, Charlotte, NC, 2012), https://www.baslibrary.org/videos/talpiot-jesus-tomb-whats-latest; James D. Tabor, "Special Session on *The Jesus Discovery: The New Archaeological Find that Reveals the Birth of Christianity* (New York: Simon & Schuster, 2012)," (lecture, Hyatt Regency, Greenville, SC, March 16, 2013).

13. Gabriel Barkay, "The Garden Tomb: Was Jesus Buried Here?" *Biblical Archaeology Review* 12, no. 2 (1986): 40-53, 56-57, https://www.baslibrary.org/biblical-archaeology-review/12/2/2.

14. Neshan Balian Jr., "The History of the Balian Family and the Armenian Ceramics of Jerusalem," https://armenianceramics.com/about/.

15. Derek Welch, "Ultra-Orthodox Exemption from Military Service in Israel Removed," *World Religion News*, September 18, 2017, https://www.worldreligionnews.com/issues/ultra-orthodox-exemption-military-service-israel-removed.

CHAPTER 10: LIVING HISTORY

1. James Bennet and Greg Myre, "In 2 Bombings, Arab Attackers Kill 13 in Israel," *New York Times*, September 10, 2003, https://www.nytimes.com/2003/09/10/world/in-2-bombings-arab-attackers-kill-13-in-israel.html.

2. Maayan Jaffe-Hoffman, "PA raises salary of terrorist who helped carry out Cafe Hillel attack," *Jerusalem Post*, September 9, 2019, https://www.jpost.com/Arab-Israeli-Conflict/16-after-Cafe-Hillel-bombing-PA-raises-salary-of-terrorist-who-murdered-7-601091.

3. "Anti-Semitism Globally," Anti-Defamation League, 2014 poll, https://www.adl.org/what-we-do/anti-semitism/anti-semitism-globally.

4. Shani Lourie, quoted in *Antisemitism*, produced by the International School for Holocaust Studies at Yad Vashem, film, 12:32, https://www.yadvashem.org/education/educational-videos/video-toolbox/hevt-antisemitism.html#729.

5. "Anti-Semitism Globally," Anti-Defamation League.

MANY THANKS TO...

...the staff and volunteers of Tel Shimron's 2019 season—especially members of Grid 33 and my roommate, Mary Perley—who loved me as a friend and not as an elder, and who soothed my aching muscles and bruised pride with Israeli ibuprofen, ice-cream bars, and hot tea.

...Dr. David Capes and Dr. Daniel Master, who made it possible for me to develop this book. If you each hadn't remembered 23-year-old me, then I might never have returned to Israel.

...the team at Harvest House, whose enthusiasm for and support of my work keeps me going when I doubt the path God has given to me.

...Bob Hawkins and Sherrie Slopianka, who enabled me to practice archaeology, write all about it, and share a sense of humor along the way.

...Kathleen Kerr, who does nothing but make my books better. You are the most talented editor I've ever worked with, and I'm so glad to call you mine!

...Andrew Langford, my first and best editor. You were unafraid to push and pull me in places where my ideas needed refinement, and this book is better because of your honesty.

...Michelle Pitts, mother of my godsons and a dearest friend. I am so proud to have you on my team, making this book better with your illustrations. I'd have chosen no one else!

...my beloved parents, Ross and Dana Womack, who bit their lips when I declared a biblical archaeology major and have only ever been proud of my work. Thank you for touring Israel with me; I'm sorry the sun and I nearly dehydrated you both!

...and my dear husband, David Haley, who used all of his many-thousand frequent flier miles to traipse through the desert with me. I'd choose no other partner, my love.

Next year in Egypt!

ABOUT THE AUTHOR

Amanda Hope Haley holds a bachelor of arts in Religious Studies from Rhodes College and a master of theological studies in Hebrew Scripture and Interpretation from Harvard University.

She maintains a blog where she encourages readers to challenge themselves to a deeper understanding of Scripture and live whole lives in community with God, family, and each other. Her podcast, *The Red-Haired Archaeologist*, is also available on her website:

http://www.amandahopehaley.com

Amanda is the author of *Mary Magdalene Never Wore Blue Eye Shadow: How to Trust the Bible when Truth and Tradition Collide* and *Barren among the Fruitful: Navigating Infertility with Hope, Wisdom, and Patience*. She cowrote *In Unison: The Unfinished Story of Jeremy and Adrienne Camp*. She contributed to The Voice Bible as a translator, writer, and editor; and she has been a content editor and ghostwriter for popular Christian authors.

Amanda and her husband, David, live in Chattanooga, Tennessee, with their scene-stealing, snuggle-loving basset hound, Copper.

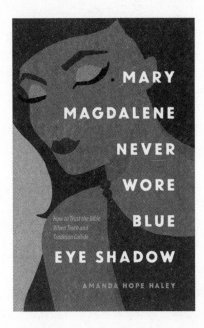

MARY MAGDALENE NEVER WORE BLUE EYE SHADOW

How to Trust the Bible When Truth and Tradition Collide

AMANDA HOPE HALEY

TRUTH, LEGEND, AND THE STORIES YOU THOUGHT YOU KNEW

Tradition suggests Mary Magdalene was a prostitute and Jesus was born in a barn. But what does the Bible really say? Armed with her theology degree, archaeological experience, and sharp wit, Amanda Hope Haley clears up misconceptions of Bible stories and encourages you to dig into Scripture as it is written rather than accept versions altered by centuries of human interpretations.

Providing context with native languages, historical facts, literary genres, and relevant anecdotes, Haley demonstrates how Scripture—when read in its original context—is more than a collection of fairy tales or a massive rule book. It's God's revelation of Himself to us.

She teaches you to...

- understand how the books of the Bible were written, transmitted, and translated

- recognize the differences between genuine Scripture and popular doctrines

- boldly seek God in His own words, ask questions of tradition, and find answers in the texts

- grow in your understanding of God and appreciation of the Bible's intimate and complex revelation of His nature

It's time to abandon the gods of tradition and meet God in His Word.

To learn more about Harvest House books and
to read sample chapters, visit our website:

www.harvesthousepublishers.com

HARVEST HOUSE PUBLISHERS
EUGENE, OREGON